Orchids
in Colour

Orchids
in Colour

Brian and Wilma Rittershausen

Photographs by
Robin Fletcher

BLANDFORD

Blandford

an imprint of
Cassell Publishers Limited
Villiers House, 41/47 Strand
London WC2N 5JE

First published 1979
First paperback edition 1984
Reprinted 1985, 1986, 1987, 1988, 1990, 1992, 1993

ISBN 0 7137 1394 1

Distributed in the United States by
Sterling Publishing Co. Inc.,
387 Park Avenue South,
New York, NY 10016-8810

Distributed in Australia by
Capricorn Link (Australia) Pty Ltd.,
PO Box 665, Lane Cove, NSW 2066

Printed in Hong Kong by Colorcraft Ltd.

Contents

AM = Award of Merit
FCC = First Class Certificate
These awards from the Royal Horticultural Society, London, are the only awards mentioned in this book.

Foreword

There is a saying, 'Those who know least, tend to burst into print'.

It is *almost* easy to write and publish a book, if you have the finances and time, as has been proved only too often by the large numbers of books found on the shelves on any given subject.

The tendency is for each new publication to be a re-hash of the previous, resulting in the perpetuation of dubious information, coupled with ill-conceived photographs.

The orchid world has produced its quota of such books in recent years. This is not meant as an outright condemnation of all orchid books published since World War II and most certainly not of the authors, it is the result of the willingness of those dedicated to the orchid cult to pass on any help and enlightenment they can to those who may wish to take up the completely absorbing hobby of growing orchids.

To a grower of orchids both privately and commercially for many years, this book has come like a long awaited breath of spring.

It is my privilege to have known Brian and Wilma Rittershausen since my earliest days in orchid growing – two people who not only have a deep appreciation of orchids and what they have to offer to those who take up their culture as a hobby, but so involved with orchids that their greatest desire is to pass on their own enthusiasm, in a way which all can understand.

The text on each genus of orchids covered is a mine of information, references are made to when specific species were introduced into Europe and from which country they came, and the variability of these species both in plant structure and flower colourings and markings.

The plant structure of each genus is graphically described, making sure we know exactly what the plant should look like in the formation of the bulbs, the pattern of foliage, the structure of flower spikes and the new growths.

One of the many unique features of this book is that, without exception, all the plants described and illustrated can be seen at any orchid exhibition, private collection, or commercial establishment. It was not the object of the authors to introduce the reader to the orchid family as something out of the ordinary, one of nature's eccentricities, and not for the average man and woman interested in the growing of plants – a reputation only too often associated with orchids.

It is understandable that many people feel a little uncertain, or even apprehensive, when orchids are mentioned, when their knowledge has been limited to a few ill-conceived photographs and scanty information.

Basically, the orchid family is a very simple form of plant, extremely adaptable to its environment, and the flower form is designed to attract the insects necessary for pollination, often to the extent of mimicry.

The flower portraits in this book are magnificently true to the subject. No photographic licence was found necessary. The photographer correctly wished to show the simple true and natural beauty as he saw it.

There is always room on the bookshelf for a book that offers such simple enlightenment enhanced with superb photography on a given subject. 'Congratulations'.

Keith Andrew
Spring, 1979

Introduction

Orchids are quite unlike other plants. As a family they stand apart, divided by their mode of growth, the formation of their flowers and their seed production. Everything about the orchids is different and perhaps this is what makes them so fascinating. They are beautiful, incredible plants which have an irresistible appeal once one has come into contact with them.

Orchids belong to one of the largest families of flowering plants. So successfully have they evolved they can be found on every continent, the only exception being Antarctica. It is understandable and, indeed to be expected, that such a successful group of plants which have spread themselves over the entire globe would present many different forms. While orchids all conform to a basic pattern, each one has evolved along different lines according to the nature of its environment. Orchids have made use of not only the insect kingdom but also spiders and humming birds in their efforts to attract successful pollinators. Among the insects all are taken advantage of, from exotic butterfly and moth to carrion fly, wasp and bee. The insect being directly related to the fragrance, which may be of sweet nectar to attract the honey bee, or rotting meat to lure the carrion fly. It will be realised that not all orchids are beautiful, although these arouse instant admiration, many are strange, curious and even ugly in the appearance of their flowers. Nevertheless, all orchids are worthy of our respect for what they represent, and many are worthy of, and receive, our unlimited adoration.

Orchids have three different methods of growth. They can be sympodial, in which the plant produces pseudo bulbs which are swollen stems. These provide the plant with a means of water storage, an adaptation to dry season climates. These pseudo, or false bulbs carry the leaves, which may consist of a single short leaf, or up to six or eight long, strap like leaves. The plant grows into a single bulb from seed, thereafter producing at least one more bulb per season, each joined by a underground rhizome, and continually adding to its size. The bulbs generally outlive the foliage by several years. With evergreen types the leaves may be shed from a bulb after the third or fourth year, the bulbs will live for several more years in this leafless state before finally dying of old age. During this time they are supporting and feeding the younger bulbs which are in leaf. Propagation is achieved by the removal of these older leafless bulbs, known as back bulbs. They can be removed by severing the rhizome and potting up individually.

Other orchids favour a monopodial type of growth in which the plant has a single upward growing stem, producing new leaves continually from the apex. These types do not propagate readily, but will occasionally produce young plants from their base, especially if the growing tip becomes damaged.

A third type of growth is shown by a few orchids and is known as diapodial. Here a series of growths are built up in a similar way to the sympodials, but lacking pseudo bulbs.

The vast majority of orchids are epiphytic, growing upon trees in forest regions, sometimes on the stoutest trunks and sometimes on the smallest twigs at the very extremities of the branches. Others cling to rocky outcrops, while the remainder, known as terrestrial, live more conventionally in the ground. This precarious epiphytic existence affords very little in the way of nourishment which the orchid has largely learnt to do without. In fact, overfeeding can be harmful to them. Their meagre needs are totally satisfied by the moisture in the atmosphere.

They thrive on humidity where other less adaptable plants would quickly perish! Those orchids which attach themselves to main branches and axils of trees derive some benefit from bird droppings washed down the bark during downpours of rain, and similarly small amounts of leaf mould which may congregate in the axils of branches and even round the bases of large orchids will help to nourish and keep moist otherwise exposed roots.

The roots of an orchid serve the plant in two ways. They will quickly adhere to anything they come into contact with, and thus form a firm anchorage to a tree. They also take up the moisture through the outer covering of the root which acts like blotting paper. Some plants will make numerous aerial roots which differ in their outer makeup from roots not similarly exposed.

Orchids are perennial plants which bloom annually provided conditions are right for them. The flowers may be produced singly on a long stem, or in a spray or branched spike. Depending upon the variety these flower spikes can be any length from a few inches or centimetres up to eight feet or $2\frac{1}{2}$ metres high. The flower spike will appear from the base of the leading bulb, while in other types it grows from the apex of the bulb. Among the monopodials the flower spike can be found inside one or other of the basal leaves, while among the diapodials, the slender stem is produced from the centre of the complete growth.

The flowers all conform, with some modification, to a basic ideal. The central structure containing the pollen masses is known as the column and also contains the stigma. This column is surrounded by three petals, two lateral petals equal in size and a third petal, known as the lip, or labellum. The lip is more often than not the most outstanding part of the flower. Often exaggerated in size, highly coloured or richly adorned, it stands out boldly from the rest of the flower, a persuasive signal to the passing pollinator which cannot be missed. The petals and lip are surrounded in their turn by three outer sepals. These may resemble the lateral petals or differ in their size and style. In a few species the sepals have become oversized and form the main attraction of the flower. Many of the east African species which are pollinated by night flying moths have segments which are more or less equal in size, including the lip. The whole flower may have no colouring other than white, combined with a strong night-time fragrance. Thus, they appeal only to the noctural insects.

When pollination has taken place, the flower collapses quickly, and fertilisation commences. The short stem immediately behind the flower becomes the eventual seed pod and this may take a period of nine to twelve months to develop. The ripening seed pod will contain many thousands of minute seeds, one of nature's extreme extravagances! Or is it? If all the seeds within one seed pod were to germinate and grow, within three generations the plants would cover the land masses of the world knee deep! This was one of Darwin's predictions. So what happens to the millions of seed floating away on the wind as they are released from the splitting seed pod? By far the vast majority are carried away on the wind and fail to germinate. A few, perhaps not one tenth of the total within the seed pod, will germinate, and of these even less will grow to adult plants.

The seed, although ready to leave the pod is extremely small and immature when compared with say, a pea, which is large by comparison and is equipped with a ready supply of green chlorophyll with which to feed the young growing plant. The orchid seed has no such food store to rely upon for its initial growth. It relies upon an outside influence in the form of microfungi, known as mycorrhiza, or root fungus. Many plants, including some of our own forest trees and heathers have a similar relationship with their own particular mycorrhiza, it is not unique to orchids. The orchid seed can only grow if it comes into direct contact with its own mycorrhiza. Once this has been achieved, the two form a symbiotic relationship, with the one becoming completely dependant upon the other for its existence. Only in this way, can orchid plants in the wild reproduce themselves. So much having been left to chance, it is essential for the continual existence of the species, that many thousands of seed are produced.

Tropical orchids were completely unknown to European civilisation until the age of travel and the great explorers set out to discover the new continents. From those early adventures were to come the first tales of orchid plants. Strange 'air plants' which grew upon the trees. They called the plants '*Epidendrums*', meaning, 'upon a tree'. In the years to follow during the latter part of the nineteenth century, explorers went specifically in search of orchids and as more and more varieties were sent back to England it soon appeared they could not all be *Epidendrums*, and the vast job of classifying each orchid which arrived in this country was undertaken. A job of work which is still going on today.

The first orchids to arrive did so in an appalling state. The result of the long sea journey, following probably many weeks of being transported through the jungles and awaiting despatch at the dock side meant that most of the orchids were dead on arrival. Those which survived were doomed to perish through lack of knowledge. However, once a few orchids had been successfully flowered, they became the wonder of all who saw them. The trickle of imported plants soon became a flood, and the first generation of orchid growers appeared, who studied the plants and their needs and built greenhouses to accommodate them. After much trial and error it became possible to cultivate and bloom tropical orchids in Britain. They became the status symbol of the wealthy, collectors were sent out in search of ever more hitherto unknown varieties. Imported plants were auctioned in London, with fabulous prices being paid for the choicest varieties. The country was swept by 'Orchidmania', the like of which had not been seen in the horticultural world since the introduction of the tulip.

Today, orchid growing has come a long way. Many plants can be happily accommodated in a small amateur's greenhouse. Where no greenhouse is available, with modern centrally heated houses and large windows affording good light, many orchids can be successfully cultivated in living rooms. While legislation closely guards the importation of orchid species from the wild, the potential grower has more variety to choose from among the hybrids of which there are today very many fine varieties the like of which would have astounded our forefathers.

For ease of classification, the orchid family is divided into botanical sections. First the tribes, which are segregated into sub-tribes. Within the sub-tribes are the various interrelated genera. Each genus contains a varying number of individual species. It is the species that are referred to by their specific names.

Many thousands of colourful hybrids have been produced, the breeding of which goes back over one hundred years. The first hybrids were the results of crossing two different species within a genus. Later, it was found that orchids would readily interbreed and it was possible to cross two related genera to produce a bigeneric cross. This was eventually taken a step further until today trigeneric and multigeneric hybrids are common place which in no way resemble the original species which make up their pedigree. The finest hybrids greatly surpass the original species in their colour, size and shape. By combining the finest qualities and strong vigour of several different plants, the modern hybrid is far easier to grow, having a wider tolerance of conditions and robustness of growth which makes it suitable for greenhouse or indoor culture.

These wonderful results with hybrids were produced firstly by sowing the seed on the surface compost of the parent plant in the hope that the mycorrhiza in the roots of the parent plant would infect the seeds surrounding it. By this method very few seedlings were germinated. In the 1920's it was discovered that orchid seeds could be germinated by using an artificial method which involved sowing in sterile flasks using a medium which contained a basic formula for germination, and thus bypassing the need for mycorrhiza. This formula contains several trace elements, mostly salts and sugars and is known as Knudson Formula 'C'. This formula formed the base for all modern flask culture. It also radically changed the production of hybrids which could now be successfully raised in far greater quantities than was thought possible. With orchids, no two hybrids are ever alike, and the varieties and variations proved endless. The next dramatic discovery to effect orchid production was that of meristemming.

Meristemming is the mass production of a single clone, or plant, to produce any number of plants which are identical in every respect to the original clone. Briefly, this is achieved by removing the meristem or growing tip from the new growth taken from the particular plant, and placing it on a growing medium as one would a seed to be germinated. The piece of meristem tissue grows and proliferates and in turn produces leaves and roots with all the appearance of a young seedling. The young meristems are grown as seedlings, taking between three to five years to reach flowering size. Following this achievement, for the first time one could purchase unflowered plants with a guarantee of the colour and shape of the flower. The most important result being that the world's finest orchids which were out of reach of most growers were now available to anyone at greatly reduced prices, according to the size of plant and colour, as one would buy a rose!

Today the culture of orchids is comparatively simple. While they grow ideally in a greenhouse where the correct conditions are more easily obtained, they will be equally happy in any living room where the same attention to their needs is catered for. It is not so important where one grows orchids, but better to have an understanding of the plants and their requirements. A greenhouse which is left unattended for many hours or days and nights can be a very dangerous place for its inhabitants. On the other hand plants dwelling indoors are under the constant eye of those around them, they will thrive far better with the extra attention of someone close at hand.

The orchids can be divided into three cultural sections. Firstly the plants which originate mostly from cool high altitudes can be grown in a minimum winter night temperature of 50° F (10° C). Those plants which come from slightly warmer growing areas of the world are classified as intermediate types, and require a minimum winter temperature of 55° F (13° C). Finally, the inhabitants of the steaming jungles, the hot house orchids, that enjoy all the heat they can get, and must have a winter night temperature of no less than 65° F (18° C). These night-time temperatures should be correspondingly higher during the summer months. The maximum temperature will depend upon the time of the year. During the winter a daytime rise of 10F° (3–4C°) on the above temperatures is desirable. During the summer months the maximum temperature in the cool house should be within 65 to 70° F (18 to 22° C). In the intermediate and hot sections, 80° F (27° C) should be the maximum. These temperatures are a guide for the different temperature range orchids. None of them should be grown colder or hotter than these temperatures indicate. It will also be seen that cool, intermediate and hot house orchids cannot all be grown successfully together.

Whichever group of orchids are grown, they all thrive on humidity. Humidity should be provided, if in a greenhouse, by soaking the floor and area beneath the staging with water, at least once a day. More in the summer during very hot spells of weather, and less during the winter, while the temperatures are lowest. The humidity should always balance with the temperature. For example, when the temperature is high, so the humidity should be equally high, and vice versa. Indoors, humidity trays can be provided for the plants which are stood on inverted saucers so as to be just above the wet gravel lining the tray.

Ventilation is important to orchids and fresh air should be supplied whenever possible, but always avoiding draughts. Indoors, plants should be carefully placed away from any draughts, and during the winter away from the direct flow of warm air and any fumes from heaters. To maintain cool night-time temperatures during the summer the ventilators may quite safely be left open during the night, which will do no harm during very warm spells.

The greenhouse will require some form of shading during the summer months to protect the plants from the direct sunshine which is liable to burn the foliage. Lath blinds placed on the outside of the glass are ideal and have the combined effect of cooling the glass and shading the plants underneath. White greenhouse paint shading can also be used to good advantage. Polythene sheeting is useful as an insulator during the winter, but should not be used for shading orchids. Coloured polythene may appear to create a good growing effect, but will cut too much light from the plants, as well as causing a rise in the inside temperature. Indoors, every advantage should be taken to get the maximum light to the plants, and there is less danger of scorching the foliage. If the plants are standing in a very sunny window, it may be necessary to employ net curtains to protect the plants without cutting too much light.

Orchids like to be kept evenly moist and should be watered regularly while they are growing. They like swift drainage and should be watered thoroughly at one application. Extremes should be avoided and the compost should not be allowed to become sodden, which will result in drowned and rotten roots. Neither should the compost become over dry. If growing plants are allowed to remain in a bone dry state for a long period, the plant will slow its growth and shrivelling of the bulbs will result. A good soaking will be needed to plump the bulbs up again.

During the winter months many orchids become dormant. When their season's growth has been completed they take a rest and will not commence any further growth until the spring. Some time during the onset of winter the deciduous varieties will shed their foliage, a clear indication that the plants are going to rest. The evergreen types will shed part of their foliage from the older bulbs. From this time onwards the plants will require little or no water until the new growth appears the following spring. Some orchids will flower during their resting period, but still require no water until the new growth is seen.

Repotting is always undertaken during the spring months of the year, when the plant is commencing its new growth and approaching the season of maximum activity, i.e. growing. The new roots which are made immediately after repotting will take full advantage of the fresh compost and being undisturbed until repotting is required again. Usually every other year is sufficient for repotting. Orchids will grow happily in a variety of composts, provided they be soil free and well drained. The compost most widely used and recommended today is bark based. The bark comes from pine trees and is graded to a suitable size. To this bark can be added a little sphagnum peat to retain moisture, with the further addition of a small quantity of charcoal to keep the compost sweet. This simple mix is all that is required for a complete, all round orchid compost. Potting is an easy process, potting as one would any other plant, but using the coarser type of compost. Artificial feeding is not essential to the successful growing of orchids, but may be applied to plants which are growing well during the summer months. If one is used to feeding plants, most types of pot plant feed is suitable for orchids, using it as either a liquid when watering, or as a foliar feed. Always taking care to use the correct dosage as recommended by the manufacturers.

Compared with other greenhouse plants, orchids have very few pests which worry them.

However, the following may occasionally be seen when steps should be taken to eradicate them as speedily as possible. There are various pest controls on the market which can be purchased from any garden supply shop. Most insecticides have a list of the pests which they control.

There are two groups of pests which attack orchids. Firstly there are those which are indigenous to orchids and may be brought into the greenhouse on infected plants. These include the sap sucking scale insects which are so called because of the scaly membrane with which they cover themselves for protection. These scale insects stick like limpets to their host and must be dislodged to be destroyed. An old toothbrush or similar is ideal for this, dipped in a solution of methylated spirit. Scale is usually found on bulbs and underneath the bracts which cover the bulbs and rhizomes. Some types can be quite persistent and will be equally at home on the exposed leaf surfaces as under the protective leaf covering.

Mealy bug is a further sap sucking pest which one may come across, usually to be found around the base of the plant, even getting down among the roots. This pest is identified by the white wooly substance with which it surrounds itself. The insect is pinkish in colour and quite easily seen. Control of mealy bug is the same as for scale insects.

Fortunately, these pests are not such a problem today as they were a few years ago. With modern insecticides which are safe and easy to use, they can be far more easily controlled. Also, stricter regulations on imported plants ensure that many of these pests do not accompany the plants into nurseries. Modern methods of control also ensure that most nurserymen for their part are able to keep their stocks in a far cleaner state than was previously possible.

The second group of pests which must be guarded against are those which gain entrance to the greenhouse from the garden outside and are therefore more common. We refer to red spider, slugs, snails, green and whitefly and occasionally springtails and other garden pests. Red spider is a minute, sap sucking mite, which can build up into large colonies on the undersides of the leaves. Their presence is usually detected by cloudy white mottling. This being the damage caused to the plant and resulting in dead leaf cells. Eventually these white areas will become infected by fungi or bacteria turning the areas black. Wiping or sponging the leaves with insecticide will have immediate control of the pest. For long term treatment regular use of a systemic insecticide will inoculate the plant against future infestations.

Greenfly can cause some damage to buds, and should be carefully washed off with water, using a small clean paintbrush for the purpose. If a few greenfly are discovered, they are almost certainly on buds, in an isolated area, and it should not be necessary to treat the whole greenhouse. While aerosols are very effective against greenfly, whitefly etc., they should not be used on buds or flower spikes. Neither should metholated spirit be used on buds, or on any plant with a soft foliage.

Slugs and snails should be kept well under control, they can cause considerable damage to tender flower spikes as well as roots and new growths. Treatment for damaged bulbs which have been eaten is to dust the affected area with powdered charcoal.

Otherwise general cleanliness in the greenhouse can do much to prevent habitation by unwanted pests. Old leaves which have been discarded by the plants should be collected and old used compost and pots not left to decay under the staging.

While there are few serious pests which attack orchids, there are even fewer diseases. Virus disease will occasionally occur on some orchids, usually encouraged by bad cultural conditions, and attacking plants which are unhealthy or weak. Sap sucking pests as previously described can also transmit virus from one plant to another. Virus disease shows up as regular black markings on the foliage. There is no cure for virus disease, although by improved culture, the plant can be grown out of it to some extent. However, it is important to stress that similar black markings can also arise through faulty culture and not virus disease. Foliage which remains for several years upon the plant may become spotted or slightly disfigured as part of the natural ageing process and is therefore nothing to worry about. The oldest leaves can be removed if they became too badly marked, provided there is sufficient remaining foliage to sustain the plant.

Cymbidiums

Cymbidiums are the most popular orchids in cultivation today. Their adaptability to grow in almost any surroundings make them an ideal beginners orchid, while their beautiful, long lasting sprays ensure their constant demand from florists and amateur growers.

The plants produce a number of well rounded pseudo bulbs, graced by an abundance of long, strap like leaves. They are evergreen plants and shed a few leaves from the oldest bulbs from time to time, particularly in the autumn. The flower spikes appear from the base of the leading bulb during the late summer months. They differ from the new growths which can appear at the same time by their round, bullet like shape. The new growths are flatter, and very soon separate into young leaves. The flower spikes continue to grow throughout the autumn, coming into bloom any time from December to April in the northern hemisphere, depending upon the variety. A mature plant may produce any number of blooms from six to twenty on a spike, this depending upon the breeding. These blooms will last in perfection for up to ten weeks, although they should be cut from the plant after about a couple of weeks. They will last just as long if kept in water. The larger the *Cymbidium*, the more flower spikes can be produced in one season. *Cymbidiums* make extensive root systems and it is not unusual for them to push themselves out of their pots when they are in need of repotting.

Cymbidiums are among the largest orchid plants in cultivation and require plenty of space in which to grow. For this reason they are better suited to greenhouse culture, rather than being grown as house plants. They require cool house conditions with a minimum winter night temperature of 50° F (10° C) rising during the day by at least ten degrees. During the summer they will require no artificial heating, when cool nights are particularly important to them. For most of the summer months full ventilation can be left on overnight allowing the plants a constant supply of fresh air. Also during this period they will require just sufficient shading to prevent scorching of the foliage. Severe yellowing of the foliage is also a sign of too much direct sunlight, while scorching will show up as ugly white patches on the exposed surfaces of the leaves. Later, the white patches will turn black brown. The plants are most vulnerable to scorching during the early spring months when the sun is gaining in its power and shading of the greenhouse has not been completed. If in doubt, a few sheets of newspaper laid over the plants will protect them until the shading is in place. From the end of the summer and for the duration of the autumn and winter months the *Cymbidiums* will enjoy all the light they can receive.

In Europe *Cymbidiums* can be grown most successfully out of doors for the summer months. If well cared for this will ensure a good hard growth and increase the flower expectation. The plants should not be removed from the greenhouse until the danger of frosts is well over. They should be placed in a position where they will receive the morning or late afternoon and evening sun, but not the midday sun, which will be too fierce for them. Ideally, they should be placed along side a wall or fence, standing on a shelf or large inverted flower pot so as to be well away from ground insects. Alternatively, the plants can be stood under a tree to afford shade, although this can cause problems with certain pests dropping from the tree onto the *Cymbidiums*. Once the ideal position has been found for them, it should be remembered that being exposed to the elements they will dry out quicker than they would in the greenhouse. Overhead spraying of the plants can be more liberal for the same reason. They should also be checked regularly against slugs and snails. By the end of the summer it will be seen that the plants have done well for their outdoor existence and flower spikes should be well in evidence. Well before the danger of early frosts the plants should be reaccommodated in the greenhouse, having first been thoroughly checked for pests.

Cymbidiums are continuously growing, merely slowing their growth during the winter. They should therefore be kept evenly moist throughout the year, with the pseudo bulbs not being allowed to become unduly shrivelled. *Cymbidiums* also enjoy regular overhead spraying during the summer, as mentioned. The summer is also the time when regular applications of liquid feed may be applied with much benefit to the formation of good sized bulbs. This feed can be phosphate or nitrate based. Many suitable brands are available in general use for other pot plants.

Black tips to the end of leaves will occasionally occur if there is something not quite to the plant's liking in one or more aspects of its culture. Any extreme such as excessively high or low temperatures, the latter possibly caused by a direct draught, will cause black tipping on the foliage. The leaves from the older bulbs which may be several years old are more susceptible to this tipping, and if on an occasional leaf can be no more than signs of old age. On the other hand should every leaf on more than one of the bulbs become affected, it is time to take a closer look at the conditions under which the plant is growing. Some small adjustment to a particular detail will in all probability remedy the complaint. For appearance sake the black tips can be neatly trimmed with a sharp knife. Always remember to clean the knife by sterilizing after use. *Cymbidiums* usually keep very free from any diseases, although should an attack of red spider be allowed to progress unchecked, this pest can transmit virus disease from one plant to another. Virus disease in *Cymbidiums* is detected by persistent and regular diamond shaped flecking which appears on the foliage. Its presence can be detected in the young growth when it shows up as a white flecking, later as the foliage ages it becomes blackened. However, more often than not odd black markings on *Cymbidium* foliage can be traced to incorrect culture, or neglect of the plant. Subsequent improved culture can grow the plant out of the black markings, although this will take several years to achieve, as the new foliage grows clean although the existing marks will not disappear.

Where conditions are right *Cymbidiums* will bloom annually quite freely. However, if the plants are growing in unsuitable surroundings, bud drop can result. Flower spikes will appear and progress normally until the buds are on the point of opening. It is at this critical stage that the buds will turn yellow and drop off, if all is not well. The most common cause of bud drop is through fumes from the heating system. In the greenhouse this may be traced to a paraffin heater and indoors through gas heating in the room. The buds, being by far the softest part of the plant are more susceptible to the slightest fumes even though the plant will remain quite unaffected. Other causes of this complaint are draughts, or the lack of direct light indoors, or too low temperatures in the greenhouse. Also a generally poor state of health of the plant. An additional cause can be over or under-watering. If severe this will also contribute to causing this condition. Once the flowers have opened satisfactorily, the main pests to watch for are the bees. Both the honey and bumble bee will pollinate the flowers if allowed entrance to the greenhouse. Once pollinated, the *Cymbidium* flower reacts immediately, and within 24 hours will collapse and die as fertilization commences.

Repotting of *Cymbidiums* is necessary every other year for mature plants, while younger plants should be 'dropped on' about every twelve months. Any repotting should be undertaken during the spring months as soon as possible after flowering. *Cymbidiums* can be grown in a variety of composts, one ideal mix being 45 % orchid bark, 45 % sphagnum peat and 10 % charcoal. These proportions are approximate and can be adjusted to suit one's particular needs. Less peat will provide a dryer compost for the grower who is heavy handed with the water can, and vice versa.

A *Cymbidium* is in need of repotting when the leading (front) bulb has reached the rim of the pot and there is no room for future growth. If the plant has pushed itself out of its pot and the roots can be seen surrounding the plant above the pot rim it is also in need of repotting. Finally, usually with young plants, a slight overall yellowing of the foliage can indicate that all the food in the compost has been used and the plant is getting insufficient nourishment. On a healthy plant the pseudo bulbs should remain in a plump state. Shrivelling of these bulbs, especially the leading ones can be the result of underwatering. The underwatered plant has had to use up its reserves stored within the bulbs when the roots have been unable to find moisture in the pot. The remedy is to drop the plant in a bucket of water and allow to soak for up to an hour. After this the bulbs will slowly plump up again over a period of about a week. Although it is difficult and unusual for a plant growing in an open bark compost to become overwatered, it may happen if the plant has been allowed to stand under a drip from a leaking roof, and the compost become sodden. In this case the roots will die, becoming brown and decayed. Without roots the plant once again has to draw upon its reserves and shrivelled bulbs will result. The overwatered plant must be removed from its pot and all the dead roots trimmed away. The rootless plant can be repotted into fresh compost and kept regularly sprayed but sparingly watered until new roots appear. The bulbs will begin to swell again immediately the new roots get under way.

As mentioned, dropping on is carried out mostly with young plants which require more room but without too much disturbance. Provided the compost is in good heart there will be no need to remove any more of it than falls away when the plant is tapped out of its pot. The roots should be seen to penetrate right down through the compost to the crocking at the bottom. They should be white and crisp with growing tips, indications of a healthy root system. Without any further disturbance the plant can be placed into a crocked pot about two inches larger and fresh compost poured in around the edge. This is pressed down with the fingers until the surface of the compost is just below the rim of the pot. *Cymbidiums* can be dropped on in this manner for a few years. Eventually all the old compost will require stripping out and dead roots which will be found in the centre of the ball must be removed. Larger plants may require dividing and the removal of some of their back bulbs.

To repot a mature *Cymbidium*, the plant must be removed from its pot and all the compost cleaned away. The majority of this will fall away as the roots are separated and pulled apart. The old dead roots can then be cut back to the base of the plant while the live roots are trimmed to a length of approximately six inches (15 cm.). Although this may entail removing about 80 % of the root system, it will greatly benefit the plant and new roots will very quickly be made taking advantage of the new compost and space within the pot. The plant may be divided where at least four good bulbs can be retained on each piece. These bulbs may include one or two without foliage. Where there are more leafless bulbs on a plant these can be removed by careful severing of the rhizome and each back bulb potted up singly. By this method *Cymbidiums* are easily propagated. Within a few weeks the back bulbs will produce new growths, the commencement of new plants, which will take approximately four years to reach flowering size. The back bulb can be left to nourish the young growing plant until it finally becomes exhausted and shrivelled. The newly repotted plant will not require watering for two to three days, allowing sufficient time for the severed root ends to dry. After this time normal watering can resume. It is not unusual for a *Cymbidium* to shrivel slightly after such an upheaval, but within a few weeks with adequate watering the bulbs will quickly plump up again as the new roots commence.

The range of *Cymbidium* species in the wild extends from the mountainous regions of the Himalayas to Australia in the south. The different varieties can be found in China, Korea and Japan, continuing through Thailand, the Phillipine Islands, Indonesia and Borneo, and covering parts of Northern Australia. They inhabit all climates from tropical to very cool. Of all the *Cymbidium* species only a few are cultivated today, mostly they have been superseded by the hybrids, which are more plentiful as well as being superior in their flowers. A number of the species which were at one time widely grown and were responsible for the commencement of what was to become long breeding lines, are sadly very rare today. Often their habitat has been destroyed or the colonies have suffered through over collecting. The species which were used mainly for breeding the first hybrids were a very small number of the showiest varieties all coming from the Himalayan region and down through Burma and Vietnam. It is from these few species such as *C. tracyanum*, *C. insigne*, *C. lowianum*, *C. eburneum*, and *C. devonianum* and *C. pumilum* among the miniature species, that we owe the remarkable range of colourful hybrids available today.

When the beginner sets out to purchase his or her first *Cymbidiums*, these will, in all probability be hybrids. The species are grown by collectors for their interest value. The beginner will more readily appreciate the fine colourings and other qualities of the hybrid. When purchasing from a reliable orchid nursery he will have the choice of buying young plants to grow on, and which will take up to three years to reach flowering size. With meristemmed varieties the colour of ones choice is guaranteed. With unflowered seedings the colour expectancy is given, as this can vary considerably. Mature plants can be purchased for a greater initial outlay, but one can be more sure of having flowers without having to wait too long.

Today *Cymbidiums* are grown throughout the world wherever the climate is cool enough, especially at night. Commercial nurseries cultivate huge quantities of plants for the cut flower trade. These enterprises succeed well in Europe, the Australian highlands and the moderate climates of South America, Africa, New Zealand and North America. Their limits being the hottest of the tropical countries. In the warmer climates they are cultivated out of doors, in lath houses built to shade them from the full sun.

Cymbidiums belong to the sub tribe *Cymbidinae*, which contains very few other genera, indicating that *Cymbidiums* have few plants which are related to them. Of these, their closest relatives are the *Cyperorchis*, which until recently were classified as *Cymbidiums*. The *Cyperorchis*, of which there are only a handful of species, will interbreed with *Cymbidiums* although the resulting cross still retains the name of *Cymbidium*. There is also on record examples of *Cymbidiums* being crossed with *Phaius* and *Ansiellia*, although these are isolated instances, and are not found in cultivation today.

Odontoglossums and other Oncidiinae

Odontoglossums are a large genus belonging to an extensive sub-tribe known as *Oncidinae*. They are a genus with many closely related genera with which they will generally interbreed. Hybrids have been produced from *Odontoglossums* from the earliest time of orchid hybridising. Today, the name *Odontoglossum* has become a term loosely used to cover a whole multitude of hybrids with a pedigree so complex that new intergeneric names have had to be found for them.

Some of the closest genera with which *Odontoglossums* have more frequently been crossed include, *Cochlioda*, *Oncidium* and *Miltonia*, to produce such man made genera as *Vuylstekeara, Wilsonara, Odontocidium* etc. All this cross breeding which has been carried through many generations of plants has produced a fantastic range of hybrids in every colour, shape and size imaginable.

In addition to the wonderful hybrids, many of the *Odontoglossum* species are available and enjoy great popularity among amateur growers. These are mainly plants of modest size, which are easy to grow and readily produce their delightful flowers at various times of the year. For their grace and charm they easily hold their own among the more flamboyant hybrids.

Odontoglossums are modestly sized plants, being easily accommodated in 5 in. (13 cm.) pots when mature. They produce stout pseudo bulbs with four or more fairly broad leaves, and make copious roots of a thin wiry texture. For this reason they like to be grown in a very open compost. An ideal mix for their needs is 60 % orchid bark, 30 % sphagnum peat, and the addition of 10 % charcoal. These proportions are approximate, and can be adjusted according to one's conditions. Repotting of mature plants is carried out every other year, provided the compost remains in a good condition for this duration This can be carried out during the spring or autumn months, depending upon the growing cycle of the individual plant. Ideally they should be repotted just as the new growth is seen from the base of the leading bulb. Many of the hybrids grow throughout most of the year. They will, however cease to grow whilst they are flowering. Some of the species have a growing season which lasts for six months only, remaining dormant for the rest of the year. Modern hybrids, however, are continuously growing except for a short period while in bloom when all the energy is diverted into the production of the flowering spike. Where good culture prevails the plant can produce and complete its annual growth within nine months. The plant follows this completed growth by flowering immediately, prior to the formation of the next new growth. Consequently, it will be seen that a well grown plant can be expected to bloom twice in every 18 months, its flowering period coming at a different season each year. This is in contrast to many of the species, which have a definite growing and resting cycle throughout the year, producing their blooms at the same time each year.

The flower spike on a typical *Odontoglossum* type hybrid will take many weeks of steady growth to produce any number of flowers up to 15 or 20, depending upon the variety. Some of the multi flowered intergeneric hybrids can easily carry hundreds of flowers on a single flower spike. This would be greatly branched, and can exceed 3 ft (1m.) high. When one takes into consideration the size of the plant, these flowering sprays are quite incredible. One must also take into consideration that these blooms are very long lived, and will last for up to three months in perfection. Undoubtedly, this puts considerable strain on the plant, and if the flower spike is left on for the whole duration of its flowering, this may impede the commencement of the next new growth. It is therefore desirable to remove the flower spike from the plant after two to three weeks, when the blooms can be kept in water where they will last just as long.

Odontoglossum hybrids have always been popular as cut flower orchids, and are excellent for use in all florists work. Their availability almost all the year round makes them an attractive proposition.

Many of the *Odontoglossum* species while evergreen, will have a decided resting period during the winter months. This entails the ceasing of growth by the plant which will require to be kept completely or partially dry until the new growth and roots commence in the following spring. Some *Odontoglossums* will bloom as their seasons growth is completed, before entering their resting period, of which *Odontoglossum grande* is one example. Others will flower immediately the new growth commences in the early spring, as *Odontoglossum citrosmum*. It is important to allow these plants a completely dry rest while they are not growing, even to the extent of allowing the oldest bulbs to shrivel slightly. This treatment coupled with maximum light to the plant will ensure a good flowering the following season.

The species within the genus *Odontoglossum* are all high altitude plants, and come from the New World. They can be found from Mexico to Peru, with the largest concentrations of them being found in Colombia, a country of vast extremes in temperature owing to its mountainous terrain. Many of the *Odontoglossums* can be found growing as epiphytes high up in the Andes range at elevations of 6,000 and 8,000 ft (2,000 and 2,500 m.) where they are often subjected to severe night time frosts. At this high altitude the air is so rarified it does them no harm. In the dryer climates of Mexico and Guatemala, other species succeed at lower elevations where they have adapted just as readily. The hybrids previously discussed have mostly been raised from the Colombian species, and it is for this reason that we grow *Odontoglossums* in conditions as light and airy as possible. Those varieties from Mexico and Guatemala which require the slightly dryer conditions make the most suitable pot plants and can be successfully grown indoors, where their cultural requirements are not difficult to achieve. The multi generic hybrids have inherited the toughness and robustness of the species and given them a tolerance which enables them to adapt to a variety of surroundings, provided their basic needs are catered for.

Odontoglossums are cool house orchids which enjoy light, airy conditions at all times. They are intolerant of heat more than anything else, and cannot cope with excessively high temperatures by day or night. During the winter months as with most orchids, they require as much light as can be given them. Their night time temperature should be no lower than 52° F (11° C), this rising during the day by at least ten degrees. This daytime temperature will vary from day to day depending upon the immediate outside weather, but should not exceed 65–70° F (18–12° C). This is easily controlled at this time of the year with the top ventilators, allowing as much fresh air to the plants whenever possible, but avoiding a draught or sudden drop in temperature. As spring approaches, there will be more opportunities of applying fresh air much to the benefit of the plants. From about the beginning of March in Britain shading of the greenhouse will be required for the duration of the summer months. This shading should not be too heavy, but just sufficient to prevent any scorching of the foliage. *Odontoglossums* are susceptible to the sun's rays and their foliage will quickly turn a reddish colour, which in itself is a good healthy sign, similar to a sun tan. However, it should not be overdone, but in moderation can improve the flowering of the plants. This tan is restricted to the hybrids, and especially some of the multi generic hybrids, although some are less affected than others. Much depending upon the breeding of the plant. During the summer months, the night time temperature should be kept as low as possible, between 52 and 55° F (10–12° C). This will mean leaving full ventilation on the plants overnight for much of the time. During the day the rise should be no more than 15° F, ideally keeping the temperature down to 65 or 70° F (18–22° C). This is quite cool for any greenhouse, particularly if it is a small one. A real boon to growing *Odontoglossums* in a small greenhouse is the installation of an extractor fan which will remove the inside air which is then replaced by fresh air being drawn in from the open ventilators thus keeping the temperature down. However, this is not always practical where a mixed collection of orchids is being cultivated, and one is trying to provide a good, all round culture for them. In this case the installation of a circulating fan will keep the air within the greenhouse moving through and around the plants, and will be of great benefit.

During the summer months the humidity of the greenhouse should be kept as high as possible during the day. This will entail regular daily damping down of the greenhouse, soaking the floor area, including corners and under staging so that all the ground is well wetted and moisture is rising during the day. The plants can be given a light overhead spray on sunny mornings, when the foliage will quickly dry. Particular attention should also be paid to the watering of the plants. Being in an open compost they can quickly become dry if not regularly checked. Ideally they should be kept evenly moist retaining the bulbs in a good plump condition. Any shrivelling of the pseudo bulbs is usually an indication of insufficient water, and this should be remedied immediately if seen. Prolonged exposure to drought during the growing season will cause *Odontoglossums* to shrivel as mentioned, which in turn will slow their growth resulting in smaller bulbs being produced, and these will be incapable of flowering.

As with other orchids, *Odontoglossums* can be lightly fed during the spring and summer months, and all the year round for those which do not stop growing. Naturally, this feed would be lessened during the winter as the plants' requirements are slowed together with their growth. This feed may be applied directly to the pots, or used as a foliar feed rosed over the plants.

Towards the end of the summer, the shading can be gradually reduced, and the plants allowed full light during most of the autumn months and throughout the winter. With the plants flowering throughout the year, it will be seen that on occasion they will appear to be a different colour when blooming during the summer or winter months. The sunlight can have a toning effect on many of the flowers, particularly the white and pastel shades, which will be darker if flowering during the winter, and slightly paler when blooming in the summer. The white hybrids from *Odontoglossum crispum*, will be much clearer in colour when blooming during the winter months. The summer flowering plant will often contain a flush of pink in the petals caused by the extra light the plants are receiving.

Where temperatures in the greenhouse rise much higher than those recommended above, and for the sake of other plants being grown there cannot be reduced, the *Odontoglossums* may well fare better by being grown out of doors for the duration of the summer months.

Here they will be able to enjoy the constant fresh air that they so desire, at the same time receiving constant good light. Extra attention will be required by plants being grown out of doors, to ensure that they do not receive too much sunlight which will result in scorching. Also that they are not allowed to suffer from underwatering. A good, hard growth can be achieved by outdoor culture, which will aid the flowering of the plants the following season. Plants which are coming into bud during the summer months would do better for being taken, if not back into the greenhouse, into a cool room indoors while their buds are developing. Out of doors they would be likely to become blotched and possibly deformed by their being exposed to the elements. Rain and wind could easily spoil their soft texture. Once indoors, a cool light position should be found for them, where they can succeed well and are not likely to experience the extremes of temperature which can occur within the greenhouse.

During the autumn and early winter months, many of the *Odontoglossum* species will be coming into their own and flowering. Those which bloom at this time will follow with their resting period, and should be allowed to become dry after flowering. Water will only be required from then on should the bulbs show signs of shrivelling. The humidity within the greenhouse will naturally be lower than during the summer, although the house should be damped down regularly to avoid dry patches occurring. Plants growing indoors for the winter can be left in a light window, but not too close to the glass, where they could be affected by a night time frost. If possible, it would be better to bring the plants into the centre of the room during the night time.

As previously mentioned, *Odontoglossums* are strong, robust plants and are not unduly worried by diseases. However, the most common cause of ailments can always be traced to extreme summer heat. This can cause a variety of complaints which appear as the plant becomes weakened by the conditions it cannot adapt to. Various markings can occur on the foliage in the form of transparent circles which later become black around the edges and can spread over the leaf. Similar watery marks can build up on the bulbs themselves, in the form of water filled bulges, here the skin of the bulb should be slit allowing the water to drain and the area dusted with sulphur or charcoal to dry the area up and prevent it from spreading. Affected plants should be given every opportunity of drying out for a period of about two weeks, during which the treated parts should have time to heal. Foliage can be painted with a powdered fungicide which has been mixed with water to produce a paste. This can be applied to both sides of the leaf.

Where good culture prevails, *Odontoglossums* keep remarkably free from pests. Probably the most persistent pest to watch out for is greenfly, which will attack the buds and sometimes the young growths of a plant. When discovered on buds, the easiest way to destroy them is to wash them off using a small paint brush and clean water. If left unchecked greenfly can greatly distort the flowers when they eventually open, as well as causing blotches on the sepals and petals.

So great is the variety to be found in *Odontoglossums*, the grower of a mixed collection of Orchids could easily give a portion of the greenhouse over entirely to them. By selecting from the multitude of species, hybrids, and multi generic hybrids which are available, one need look no further for a greater variety of plants! In addition to the charm of the species many of them have the added attraction of a sweet fragrance which makes them even more desirable. Among the hybrids and their varying flowering times, one would never be without flowers.

Paphiopedilums

Of all the plants to be found within the orchid family, the *Paphiopedilums* stand apart. They are a curious branch of the orchid family separated botanically by their having two stamens instead of the usual one. They belong to a tribe which is divided into four sub tribes. These include the *Cypripediums*, which are herb like plants growing as terrestrials. They thrive in moderate climates and often grown as alpine plants. A small, not generally cultivated genus are the *Selenipediums* which come from South America and produce tall, reed like plants. *Phragmipediums* are an interesting genus from Central and South America, which are not extensively grown owing to the difficulty of procuring them.

Paphiopedilums remain the most important genus within this group, being very popular and widely grown. The species originate from the far east, covering India and China, spreading down through the islands of the East Indies. They are varied in their mode of habitat and may be found as terrestrials growing in the loamy humus found beneath forest trees, or shallow rooting in grass and shrublands. They also occur on outcrops of mossy rocks and occasionally as epiphytes. *Paphiopedilums* are bulbless orchids, producing instead a number of growths from a single underground rhizome. Their foliage is always attractive to the eye and may be a light glossy green, or beautifully mottled or marbled with darker shades of grey and green. The flower stem is produced from the centre of the mature growth and may carry a single flower, or less often, several flowers, depending upon the variety. This stem may be barely an inch or $2\frac{1}{2}$ cm high with the flower nestling atop the growth, or nearer three feet or one metre high. The *Paphiopedilums* propagate readily by division when large enough. However, some varieties are best left for as many years as possible without splitting which can reduce the strength of the plant. The most robust and therefore faster growing types can be regularly divided into plants consisting of two or three growths.

The flowers are unique, their main feature being the characteristic pouch giving rise to this orchid's popular name of 'Ladies Slipper'. The typical *Paphiopedilum* has a predominant dorsal sepal and two lateral petals. The two lower sepals are usually fused into one, which is more or less hidden by the pouch, a modification of the more usual lip or labellum. In some species, particularly among the *Phragmipediums*, the lateral petals become the most spectacular features of the flower *Phragmipedium caudatum* for example extends its lateral petals to a length of 30 in (76 cm). These are much shorter when the flower opens, but within a week, growing at a rate of half an inch or over 1 cm a day, twisting in their length as they extend downwards, they rapidly attain their great length. When the petal tips are extended horizontally this extraordinary orchid qualifies as being the world's largest flower. A few *Phragmipedilums* are grown today by collectors, these are mostly the species, while a very few hybrids are in cultivation.

Extensive hybridising has been carried out with *Paphiopedilums* from before the turn of the century. Indeed, some of the earliest hybrids raised are still in cultivation today. While it was found that *Paphiopedilums* would readily interbreed, the amount of seed produced from a seed pod was surprisingly small compared with the average amount of seed produced by most other orchids. Also, they proved to be very slow to germinate and grow and it was for these reasons that the hybridising of *Paphiopedilums* took many years to achieve a similar standard as other hybrids. With the introduction of modern seed raising techniques, the production of hybrids was greatly speeded up, although there was still the problem of very little seed in most of the pods. This makes many of the hybrids all the more sought after, where only a handful on one cross exists. The primary hybrids which were first produced showed little variation on their two parents, but gradually as their breeding became more and more complicated, the flowers became larger, rounded and more heavily textured, until today we have in the average *Paphiopedilum* hybrid a huge flower well rounded and with tremendous texture and gloss. The colours have been greatly intensified into gleaming reds, coppers, bronzes and yellow greens in many hues. In sharp contrast are the soft powdery whites and rosy pinks of the latest breeding lines.

To date *Paphiopedilums* have defied all attempts to meristem them, and their only method of propagation is still by division.

Many of the *Paphiopedilum* species which, up to a few years ago, were so plentiful are now scarce in the wild, and indeed some of them have probably become extinct, such has been the over-collection or destruction of their habitat. *Paphiopedilum* species purchased from orchid nurseries today may well be plants which have been raised in cultivation. Unlike some orchids where the original species are small compared with the modern hybrids and therefore only of botanical interest, all the *Paphiopedilum* species are extremely handsome and all are worth cultivating alongside the hybrids. The species can be divided into different temperature groups depending upon which part of the globe they come from. Most of the varieties from India and China can be successfully cultivated in the cool house, with a minimum temp. of 50°F (10 °C) while those types from the Malayan peninsula including the Philippines and down to Borneo require intermediate to hot house conditions with a minimum temp. of 55°F (14 °C) to 65 °F (18 °C). The majority of the modern hybrids, which have a considerable mixture of species in them are at their best when grown in fairly hot conditions.

There has always been a great interest in *Paphiopedilums* as cut flower orchids, and in years gone by selected forms of the variety *P. insigne* were grown in their thousands to supply the demand for their cut blooms. Their ease of culture and tolerance of more or less any type of compost combined with their meagre heat requirements, made them an ideal proposition for the commercial grower, who may have had no other experience with orchids. The flowering time of these orchids commences in the northern hemisphere in December and with the blooms lasting a good eight or ten weeks in perfection, this season was extended well into the spring months, covering Christmas and the duller months when these exotic blooms were in greatest demand. So tough was the endurance of these plants they were cultivated for many decades with little or no attention, continually increasing in size. Often these plants would reach a stage in their growth where they made very little new root, but supported themselves entirely by the older growths on the plant. Drastic disturbance such as dividing and repotting would give such plants a tremendous shock from which many would not recover! In more recent years the role of *Paphiopedilums* has been as house plants where again they show their considerable versatility by adapting to indoor living with a vigour which has earned them their tough reputation.

It is not so easy with *Paphiopedilums* to define them by particular colours as one can do with other orchids. Their colourings are so often a combination of browns, purples, pinks and greens, overlaid on the petals in limitless stripes and veins, spots and dots. Very few of the flowers are self coloured, and those which are are more often concolor or albino forms of the type. Whether it is this extraordinary intricate colouring of the flowers, or their unique shape and structure which fascinates and draws people to them, it is difficult to say, but *Paphiopedilums* have always stood high on the list of popular orchids while other varieties have gained and lost favour among growers the world over.

Paphiopedilums do not make extensive root systems and being mainly terrestrial do not have to cope with aerial roots. The roots are made sparingly and are covered with a thick growth of hairs. For this reason their compost need not be quite so open as for may other orchids. While we recommend the use of a bark based compost which suits them well, to this can be added up to 50% sphagnum peat, or if obtainable, a fibrous loam. The extra addition of 10% charcoal is of great benefit in keeping the compost sweet. The plants will require repotting about every other year, when they should be retained in as small a pot as possible. One should bear in mind their meagre rooting system when potting on. At repotting time which is best undertaken in the spring, preferably when the new growth is showing, very little root trimming should be necessary. The plants should be allowed to 'sit' on top of the compost, with the base of the plant on a level with the rim of the pot. No part of the plant above the roots should be buried in the compost as this can lead to rotting of the new growth. If large enough, the plants can be divided provided one leaves at least three good growths on each plant. Otherwise, the plant can be left in one clump to be grown on into a specimen plant. *Paphiopedilums* are modestly sized plants, and without the heavy encumberance of pseudo bulbs are quite easy to lift and handle, and therefore the grower is encouraged to grow the plant as a single specimen. In this way a large mature plant consisting of several growths can produce as many flowers each year, greatly adding to its appeal.

Paphiopedilums do not have a resting period, neither do they have any means of storing up water for long periods. For these reasons the plants should be regularly watered and the compost kept evenly moist throughout the year. It is important that the two extremes of underwatering and overwatering should be carefully avoided. An underwatered plant will quickly show signs of suffering as the leaves lose their texture and become limp. A similar state will occur with the overwatered plant after the loss of the roots by drowning. When watering *Paphiopedilums*, care should be taken not to allow water to become lodged inside the growths. If this occurs frequently, particularly during the winter months, it can cause rotting of the growth. This will be seen by the brown and wet appearance of the leaf or leaves at their base. All rotting parts should be carefully removed, and the area dusted with sulphur. If the crown of the plant remains unaffected, there is a good chance that the plant will grow again. For the same reason *Paphiopedilums* should seldom, if even, be sprayed overhead with water. Any buds which inadvertently get wet, should be carefully dried immediately to avoid spotting or rotting of the flower.

Being shade loving plants, *Paphiopedilums* make excellent house as well as greenhouse plants, and can be grown to perfection in either place. During the summer they should be carefully shaded from the direct sun, although the light should not be reduced on them, while almost full light can be given throughout the winter months. The shading should be applied early in the year so as to avoid any unnecessary scorching of the foliage.

Ventilation can be applied freely during the summer months, how much depending upon the varieties and where they are being grown. As with all orchids, they dislike cold draughts.

Paphiopedilums remain remarkably free from pests and where good growing conditions prevail there are very few pests which will harm them. Scale insects may make an unwanted appearance possibly being transferred to them from another plant standing close by. This pest is easily controlled with a systemic insectide.

Their temperature requirements can vary as mentioned depending upon where they originate. In many instances the species prove to be easier than the hybrids to grow often requiring cooler conditions. The green leaved Indian species do well when grown in the cool house. They will be quite at home alongside many other orchids which require the same treatment. The mottled leaved varieties are those which require slightly higher temperatures. These do well in the intermediate section, or warm room. An indoor growing case is often ideal for these plants, which are attractive to look at when not in bloom. The larger growing, green leaved varieties from the Philippines will also grow with the mottled varieties, but can become considerably larger perhaps more suited to the greenhouse where there is more room for them. The majority of hybrids grow better in slightly warmer conditions and again do well in indoor growing cases. The marbled leaved varieties are smaller growing with a charm all their own. They are mostly white flowered, with a few pale yellow and pink types, all coming from south east Asia. These plants are more delicate and slower growing than their larger cousins, and they do best in a shady part of the hot house. They may be successfully grown alongside the *Phalaenopsis*, but in slightly dryer conditions.

Phalaenopsis

Among the hot house orchids *Phalaenopsis* head the list for popularity. This status has been achieved by the grace and beauty of their flowers which appear on elegant sprays and last for many weeks. These blooms will appear at various times of the year, there being no definite season for the flowering of hybrids. While the colours are somewhat restricted to pink and white, within this range there can be found an enormous variety of shades, with lip markings and colourations which give as wide a variety as can be found in any genus. They are most rewarding orchids to grow in a hot greenhouse or warm room where they will bloom freely with great frequency.

Phalaenopsis are a genus of orchids known as Monopodials, referring to their method of growth. Unlike the majority of orchids, they do not produce pseudo bulbs, but grow from a single rhizome from which new leaves are continually being produced at the apex. These leaves are thick and fleshy and very broad. The old leaves are shed at the rate of one or two a year, often during or just after flowering. These are always replaced by the younger leaves and an average plant will retain between three to six leaves at any time. *Phalaenopsis* do not readily propagate, but young plants or 'keikis' can sometimes be produced by cutting back the flowering spike to a lower node which will encourage the growth of a young plantlet. These plantlets should be left on the plant until they have produced their own roots and can be potted up independently.

Phalaenopsis are epiphytic by nature and cling to the tree trunks with stout, flattened aerial roots, which will grow to several feet in length and are covered with a silvery velame. These roots will adhere very strongly to the tree surface, and are required to hold the considerable weight of a fully grown plant. The long, broad leaves will assume a pendent habit in nature: which is an advantage with the heavy leaves and also prevents water from lodging inside the new leaf, which can plague plants grown upright in pots. In some species the foliage is plain green while in others the leaves are beautifully mottled with broken bars of silvery grey and lighter green.

The *Phalaenopsis* are related to an emourmous group of orchids which include *Vandas*,

Renantheras and *Doritis*. They are widely distributed throughout the far east and have spread from India to New Guinea. The majority of species which are grown today and which are responsible for most of the early breeding of *Phalaenopsis* hybrids come from the Philippines and neighbouring islands. Unlike most of the genera to which *Phalaenopsis* are related, they are shade loving plants, which makes them easier to cultivate and flower in the northern hemisphere. It also renders them suitable for indoor culture, where they grow very successfully in indoor growing cases where the high temperature and humidity they require can be easily maintained at little cost. Their relatives among the *Vandas* on the other hand are sun loving plants, which succeed best in full continuous sunlight. Unfortunately, these conditions simply cannot be achieved in Britain, and for this reason only a few *Vandas* and their allies are grown. However, *Phalaenopsis* will interbreed with *Vandas* to produce the bigeneric genus of *Vandaenopsis*, as also *Doritaenopsis*, produce by crossing *Phalaenopsis* with *Doritis*. There are a number of other interesting and beautiful bigeneric crosses being made with *Phalaenopsis*, but these are grown in sunnier climates and they do not flower so freely in Britain.

From a relatively few of the large flowered Philippino species including *P. sanderana, P. stuartiana, P. schillerana* and *P. amabilis*, hybridising was commenced before the end of the last century with such success that before long there were many hundreds of *Phalaenopsis* hybrids listed. However, because of very close interbreeding, many of the hybrids were exactly alike in their colouring. In an effort to produce different colours and patterns into *Phalaenopsis* they were crossed with the smaller flowered species such as *P. lueddemanniana* and its varieties. This species carries much smaller flowers, star shaped with a heavier texture to the petals and sepals. The flowering habit is also different, and a few blooms are produced at a time from a continuously growing spike producing a succession of flowers over several months. Among the *P. lueddemanniana* type species are to be found richer colourings and markings, as well as the elusive yellow, which has kept hybridisers busy for generations trying to recapture it in the larger hybrids. From this interesting line of breeding come a number of novelty crosses: hybrids which are part way between the larger and smaller growing types. Into the hybrids come such sought after additions as spots on the sepals and petals, evenly distributed over the flower's surface and greatly adding to the flower's appeal. A further breeding line has been carried on by crossing with *Doritis pulcherrima*. This has generally increased the number of flowers on a spray, which may be smaller, but much brighter in their colouring. The influence of the *Doritis* will also encourage a tall upright flowering spike.

Where sufficient warmth can be given them *Phalaenopsis* make highly successful cut flower orchids. They are grown extensively in North America for this purpose as well as house plants. In Europe there is an equally high demand for them, where the white varieties are grown to be dyed in yellow and blue. Apparently, these colours are most popular and the effect is achieved by placing the cut stems into coloured water before marketing. This of course, is not exclusive to orchids and is carried out successfully on other cut flowers such as Carnations

Today both hybrid and species *Phalaenopsis* are grown, the latter usually by the collector. The beginner will find the hybrids more immediately pleasing to the eye, and owing to the high cost of importing plants form the Philippine Islands, the hybrids can often be raised from seed at less cost. In addition to which the plants can be flowered within three to four years from seed, thus keeping down the price. Also, in many cases, the hybrids are more robust and tolerant of inexperienced treatment. While the species have definite flowering seasons, usually spring or autumn, the hybrids due to their interbreeding can flower almost all the year round. *Phalaenopsis* also have one further attraction. When the first spray of flowers has finished, the spike can be cut back to a lower node on the stem, and from this node a secondary spike will grow to give a further spray of flowers. However, this should only be done on mature plants who have the strength and ability to carry the extra blooms. It is not unusual for large, mature plants to carry such a flower spike for several months, during which time it can be cut back more than once to produce more and more flowers. However, these flowers will become reduced in size and quality on the secondary spikes. By this time the plant may already be showing a new flower spike and this will be in bloom by the time the old flower spike is removed altogether. Thus it can be seen that a mature plant can remain in bloom almost continually for a period of twelve months or more. Such plants should be given a resting period from continuous flowering if they show the slightest signs of strain, such as the loss of texture from the foliage or the loss of more than one leaf at a time. Should this happen, all flower spikes should be removed at their base until the plant has grown one or two new leaves to build up its strength again. Being without pseudo bulbs these orchids have little means of storing up energy.

The most important single factor in the culture of *Phalaenopsis* is warmth. They are essentially hot house orchids which revel in as much heat as can be given. Ideally, their minimum night temperature should not drop below 70 °F (20 °C) although an occasional drop to 65 °F (18 °C) for just a few hours during very severe winter weather will do them little harm. This nightime temperature should rise during the daytime by at least ten degrees, and fifteen or twenty degrees higher during warm summer days. These high temperatures must always be balanced by a correspondingly high humidity within the greenhouse or growing case, and damping down will be necessary at least once a day.

While ventilation is supplied freely with most orchids, with the *Phalaenopsis*, while it is necessary to maintain a good buoyant atmosphere, fresh air from the ventilators must be applied sparingly, usually restricted to hot summer days. *Phalaenopsis* are very sensitive to pollution in the air and can be all too easily damaged by gas or paraffin fumes where these forms of heating are installed. It is therefore important to growing *Phalaenopsis* successfully that a circulating fan be installed which will keep a movement of air through and around the plants. The fan will be at its greatest advantage when placed at staging level so that the air can flow through the plants themselves, to the extent that the flowering spikes can be seen to be waving slightly in the breeze. Such a fan can be kept running permanently over the plants, night and day. It is important that only air of greenhouse temperature should be moved through the plants in this way. Where hot air fan heaters are installed, these should of course, be placed low down on the floor and not used in close contact with the plants, unless the heat be turned off.

Shading of the *Phalaenopsis* should be completed early in the spring. This shading will be quite heavy, and as a guide one should be able to look at the sun through the glass without it hurting the eyes. The shading may be in the form of paint or blinds, combined with a netting placed on the inside or outside of the glass. In the *Phalaenopsis* house it is less important to keep temperatures down, but rather to prevent too much direct sun from reaching the foliage. Although the foliage is thick and apparently tough, it is also very fleshy and can be easily scorched by too much sun. For this reason the shading is retained until quite late in the autumn, when there is far less power in the sun. During the winter *Phalaenopsis* can have almost full light, but it is as well to retain a little shading on the glass even at this time of year.

The watering requirements of *Phalaenopsis* are direct and simple. They should be allowed sufficient water throughout the year to keep the compost in a continually moist condition.

Most *Phalaenopsis* produce copious roots, many of them outside the pot, and these will absorb much of their moisture through the humidity within the greenhouse or growing case. *Phalaenopsis* are continuous growers, and while their growth will slow considerably during the winter months in accordance with the lack of daylight hours, they have no resting period and cannot cope with long spells of drought. Feeding can be given to *Phalaenopsis* all the year round, again reducing the frequency during the winter when growth is at its slowest.

An ideal compost for *Phalaenopsis* should be very open to allow free drainage through the pot. Although they make extensive root systems *Phalaenopsis* should not be overpotted, and half pots are preferable to deep pots. As mentioned many of the roots will be made outside the pot rim and one should not attempt to insert these aerial roots into the compost. When repotting, which should be done annually, aerial roots should be allowed to remain outside the pot. A bark based compost is most suitable for *Phalaenopsis* with the addition of up to 50% sphagnum peat. While annual repotting is beneficial, often one can merely remove the compost within the pot by taking it out with the fingers, and leaving the plant inside the pot. This is easily done where the plant is firmly adhering to the inside of the pot by its roots. Because of the way in which *Phalaenopsis* grow particularly the species, they lend themselves easily to 'novelty' potting. By this we mean that they can be grown successfully on rafts, or in baskets. Suspended from the roof of the greenhouse or against the back of an indoor growing case. When wired onto pieces of cork bark with the leaves in a downward position, they not only grow well in this position, they make a most attractive looking plant. Within a few months a newly mounted plant will have produced a number of aerial roots which will have adhered strongly to the bark. The wire supports can then be removed leaving the plant self supporting on the bark. When placing a plant on bark in this way it should be removed from its pot and all compost shaken off. Any dead roots should be removed and live roots treated with care not to snap them. A piece of bark should be selected which will allow plenty of room for the roots to adhere to. While placing the plant in the centre of the bark, a small amount of osmunda fibre or sphagnum moss can be placed carefully around the base of the plant, covering the roots which were inside the pot. Any aerial roots can be left uncovered. The whole is then wired firmly to the bark taking care to bring the wire across the very base of the plant and not to cut into the fleshy green part. Any *Phalaenopsis* can be grown in this way, although the species are usually more easily adaptable. Once a plant is being grown on bark it will require more frequent waterings, and may be lightly sprayed during the summer when there is no danger of water lodging inside the new leaf.

Phalaenopsis have very few pests to which they are prone. Their protective, thick fleshy leaves are usually enough to deter pests which attack other orchids. However, in the hot humid climate, it is an ideal breeding ground for slugs, and these pests can eat a surprisingly large area of new leaf in just one night. They should always be kept at bay. Diseases of *Phalaenopsis* can usually be traced to incorrect culture. Exposure to cold for example can cause a number of ugly markings on the foliage, as the leaf cells suffer and die producing blackened areas on the surface of the leaf. These areas should be powdered with sulphur or a powdered fungicide to prevent them spreading, although in severe cases they can cause the loss of the leaf. Cold, combined with damp are the worst enemies of *Phalaenopsis*, and this combination can cause a leaf or part of the leaf to become transparent and very wet. This can happen overnight and quickly spread through the plant if not checked. A plant with only three or four leaves can quickly succumb, and collapse as the rot sets in. Again the remedy is to dust with sulphur, having first dried off the leaf, releasing any water under the surface if necessary. As mentioned, water should never be allowed to lodge inside the young leaf at the centre of the plant. This can all too quickly set up a rot, which can cause the loss of the plant. If treated in time, and only the growing tip of the plant is lost, a new plant will start to grow from the base, thus saving the life of the plant. However, this new plant will take a further three or four years before it will be capable of flowering. Therefore every care should be taken to protect the growing tip of the plant. One complaint to which *Phalaenopsis* are prone is bud drop. This occurs when the buds which have been growing well are about to open. At this stage they turn yellow and drop off with a dried shrivelled appearance. There are a number of causes of this, the most common one being where paraffin or gas heaters are used in the greenhouse. Other reasons for the same complaint are the lack of air movement within the house or case, and during the winter months, the lack of light during prolonged spells of dull rainy weather. The solution is to reduce the flower spike to a lower node, and await the formation of new buds. In the meantime taking a long look at ones conditions to determine where the trouble lies.

Cattleyas and other Laeliinae

Cattleyas are a genus of epiphytic orchids belonging to a large sub tribe known as Laelinae. They are among the most beautiful and flamboyant of all orchids, and are certainly the largest flowered plants to be covered in this book. Together with their allied plants they come from tropical South America, with a number of the species to be found north of the Panama Isthmus up to Mexico. They are very closely related to *Laelias, Brassavolas (Rhyncholaelias)* and *Sophronitis* with which they will readily interbreed producing the multi generic hybrids which have made an important contribution to orchid hybridising the world over.

Cattleyas produce stout, robust plants, with club shaped pseudo bulbs and one or two thickly textured leaves, which are retained on the plant for several years before being discarded. By their leaves the *Cattleya* species can be divided into two groups. Those which carry a single leaf per bulb are known as the unifoliates, while other varieties which produce two leaves per bulb are known as the bifoliates. The unifoliates usually produce the larger and softer flowers, while the bifoliates have smaller, slightly heavier textured flowers, and more on a stem. With generations of interbreeding between these two groups, these distinctions have become merged in the hybrids. *Cattleyas* will readily produce more than one new growth in a season enabling them to grow into large specimen plants within a few years. In addition they will propagate rapidly, almost every bulb showing a dormant eye at its base from which it will grow if severed from the main plant. In the wild *Cattleyas* will grow into huge clumps several feet or over a meter in size, and weighing several lbs. or kgs. Their stout pseudo bulbs by which they are often weighed down are capable of retaining sufficient moisture from their growing season to carry the plants safely through the long dry season in the regions where they grow.

Cattleyas produce an abundance of roots, many of these extending over the rim of the pot. Those which are inside the pot will adhere very strongly to the sides, often making it difficult not to damage them when repotting. If badly damaged, these roots are better removed altogether. The flowers appear, depending upon the variety, mainly during the spring or autumn months from the apex of the pseudo bulbs, when they will last up to three weeks on the plant. The small, developing buds are produced inside a protective sheath. The sheath covering enables the young buds to develop safely until they are almost fully grown, at which stage they completely fill the sheath which splits to allow the buds to emerge and open into full flower. Depending upon the variety the plant may carry anything from a single flower, more often two to three, up to six flowers on a stem.

The most predominant colours to be found among the *Cattleya* alliance are the rich glowing purples and mauves, the reds and soft pastel pinks. These in sharp contrast to the glistening whites and clear yellows. More recent specialised lines of breeding have produced the elusive green and blue shades. While these latter colours are greatly in demand for their originality they are not so plentiful and can be costly to purchase.

A further attraction of the *Cattleyas* is that many of them, the species as well as the hybrids, are highly perfumed – an attribute rare among orchid hybrids.

All the species within this and allied genera are extremely beautiful. Since they were first introduced to Britain during the latter part of the last century they have been in constant cultivation, and they have lost none of their popularity through the extensive breeding of hybrids which has been carried on at an amazing rate since that time. Today, so many of these delightful species are sadly very rare and impossible to obtain. Any species found in cultivation are plants which have been artificially raised in an attempt to prevent them becoming extinct. The plants more generally found in collections are modern hybrids which are many times removed from the original species. The term '*Cattleya*' is loosely applied to all the intergeneric hybrids within the sub tribe. There are in fact, very few pure *Cattleya* hybrids grown. The average hybrid is an intergeneric cross including *Laelia* and *Brassavola* (*Rhyncholaelia*), *Sophronitis* and more rarely some of the allied plants such as *Epidendrum*, *Diacrium* etc., have been successfully used to produce even more variations of these beautiful plants.

Over the decades *Cattleyas* have proved to be extremely tolerant plants which can be grown in almost any climate. In the tropical countries they enjoy the hot humid conditions and can be grown with great ease, thriving on the humidity constantly available to them. In cooler climates they adapt most successfully to greenhouse culture with artificial heating during most of the year. They are probably more widely grown throught the world than any other orchid.

Cattleyas make ideal cut flower orchids. Many commercial growers raise them by the thousand for their cut blooms highly prized by any florist. *Cattleya* blooms are far more sensitive to light than other orchids. They will respond to controlled artificial lighting and can be timed to come into flower for any particular day. This is done extensively in Europe and the USA.

In Britain *Cattleyas* are grown successfully indoors and in greenhouses. They are termed intermediate orchids and require a minimum winter night temperature of 55 °F (14 °C) with a substantial daytime rise. This minimum temperature should be a few degrees higher in the summer indicating that artificial heating will be required for all but a few months during the summer.

Ventilation which is important to all orchids should be applied readily whenever possible, avoiding a sudden drop in temperature. To maintain the higher temperature the *Cattleyas* will be the last to receive fresh air in the morning, and the first to be closed down for the night. This slight restriction of fresh air will enable the grower to maintain a higher humidity around the plants, which will greatly benefit the *Cattleyas*. They should be kept regularly damped down, this often being done after the ventilators have been closed for the day. A slight overhead spray can be given to the plants during the summer months while they are growing and while their aerial roots are most active. This spraying should not be so heavy as to allow water to run into a half completed growth where it could cause the new growth to rot.

During the summer months *Cattleyas* should never be allowed to become dry. They should be watered regularly, soaking the compost in one application and kept evenly moist. This will ensure a constant rate of growth by the plant which should complete its bulb by the autumn and produce its flowers at that time, after which it will commence to rest for a period of three to four months. While the plant is at rest watering should be considerably reduced and possibly withheld altogether. Provided the pseudo bulbs remain plump no water will be necessary. Should the bulbs show signs of shrivelling the *Cattleyas* may be given one good watering to plump them up, and no water again unless required. Once the new growth can be seen to be on the move at the base of the plant, normal watering can be resumed, as also the light overhead spraying.

Shading of the *Cattleyas* should begin early in the spring, bright sunlight can quickly cause scorching of their foliage. It should be retained throughout the summer months until the autumn, when full light can be given them for the winter.

When the new growth has started, the new rooots will follow in a short time. It is at this stage when the new growth is showing and before the new roots have started that the plants should be repotted if required. *Cattleyas* should be repotted every two to three years, when the leading bulb is over the rim of the pot and the new growths are being made outside of the pot. Their compost should be very open to allow free movement of their thick fleshy roots, and swift drainage which is important for the health of these roots. A bark based compost suits then well, of a coarse grade, and the pots should be well crocked at their base. Propagation and division of *Cattleyas* can be done on a regular basis, the plants often becoming large enough to divide every two or three years. *Cattleya* bulbs are joined by a very stout rhizome which is clearly visible on the surface of the pot. When dividing or propagating from a plant, it is advisable to severe this rhizome where required during the autumn after the seasons growth has been completed. The plant is then left undisturbed in its pot for a further six months. In the spring when the plant once again commences its growth, the bulb immediately behind the severed rhizome will also start to grow, thus providing an independant plant. This method of propagation will ensure that the rear portion of the plant starts its growth earlier in the season, at the same time as the growth on the leading bulb. If flowering divisions are required each plant should consist of at least four good sized bulbs. If pieces are reduced smaller than this, down to single bulbs, these will take three to four years to reach flowering size.

Repotted plants should be given sufficient room in their new pots to allow for at least two years future growth. This can be helped by positioning the plant to one side of the pot. Once the new roots can be seen to be growing from the base of the new growth, the plant can be fed at regular intervals for its growing season. This feed can be applied about every third watering.

As the growth advances during the summer months, the developing bulb becomes heavier and may assume a near horizontal position. A supporting cane can be inserted close to the bulb to which it can be tied, or, provided the previous bulb is sufficiently stout, it may be used to support the new bulb. In this way the plants can be kept in a neat growing formation, and it avoids their becoming top heavy in their pots. An upright bulb is also an advantage when the plant comes into flower, when extra staking of the blooms which overlap each other can improve the position and appearance of them. When the flowers have finished the stem should be cut not too close to the bulb. The stem is considerably thick and fleshy and to prevent the possibility of rot setting in, the severed end should be carefully dusted with powdered charcoal or sulphur to dry up the cut as soon as possible.

Most greenhouse pests will not harm *Cattleyas* owing to the thick texture of their leaves. However, their bulbs are covered with a protective sheath which is green while the bulb is growing and quickly dries out after the bulb has matured, remaining on the plant in a dried state. This covering makes an ideal home for scale insects, which can remain undetected and build up into large colonies. There are a number of different scale insects, any of which can cause considerable harm to *Cattleyas* and should always be looked out for. Some will congregate around the rhizome and roots of the plant, where they can kill the embryo growths of the plant, and in doing so lead to the death of the whole plant. Other may remain on the leaf surface. Whenever their presence is suspected, all protective sheathing should be removed from the bulbs and rhizomes and the whole plant cleaned with Methylated Spirit or Jeyes Fluid to destroy the present population. Further, long term control can be achieved with the use of a systemic insecticide. Where the pest has been cleaned away the plant may show yellow or brown patches. These patches cannot be removed, but will not spread once the pest has been eradicated. Mealy bug is a further pest to attack *Cattleyas*, when their detection and treatment is the same as for scale insects.

Another problem which can affect *Cattleyas* is bud drop or premature spotting of their flowers. Owing to the soft texture of *Cattleya* blooms, they are susceptible to bad air. Pollution in the form of heating fumes can cause the buds to turn yellow and drop off. Mostly this will occur when the buds have emerged from their sheath, but occasionally it may happen, in this case through cold or overwatering, while the buds are still inside the sheath. If the buds do not appear to be developing inside the sheath, it can be carefully peeled down each side to reveal the buds for inspection. If they are green, all is well. Otherwise they may appear dark brown and soggy, and should be removed immediately. The end of the stem should be dusted and the sheath removed to allow the area to dry out. *Cattleya* flowers which successfully open but become spotted or streaked with black markings after they have been open a few days, can be suffering from cold, wet or lack of fresh air. Keeping the plants which are in flower in dryer conditions and reducing the watering of them can assist the flowers to remain longer in their prime. Bright sunlight can also be harmful to the blooms, which should be kept in a shady position.

Cattleyas are among the most successful of orchids to be meristemmed. There is a tremendous range of exciting colours and combinations from which the potential grower can select the very best quality of their choice. Unflowered seedlings can also be obtained at ease with the added excitement of not knowing exactly what colour a flower is going to be.

Cymbidium eburneum

This was at one time a very popular and widely grown species, being extremely plentiful before the age of hybrids. The plant comes from northern India where it grows at elevations of 5 to 6,000 ft ($2\frac{1}{2}$–3000 m) in the Himalayas. It was first introduced into Great Britain in 1846. The plant has a compact, tufted type of growth with elongated pseudo bulbs supported by numerous narrow leaves. It blooms in the middle of the *Cymbidium* season during February and March in Europe. The flower spike can carry one, two or rarely three, highly fragrant flowers. This *Cymbidium* was one of the first to be used by the hybridisers who were quick to realise its potential as a parent. Indeed many of the resulting hybrids were outstanding for their time. The species proved to be very predominant over its progeny and some very fine white hybrids have been produced directly from *C. eburneum* over the years. Today, the vast majority of white *Cymbidiums* trace their ancestry back to this species.

C. eburneum is still available from some nurseries today. However, imported plants which are received are always very poor specimens which take several years to grow and establish themselves. *C. eburneum* no longer graces the small amateur's mixed collection, but is found only occasionally where it is considered a collector's item and highly prized.

The plant likes to be grown to a large specimen when it will flower freely and can be admired in its full beauty. Unfortunately, such specimens are rarely seen today, although they were a common sight in England around the turn of the century and for many years after.

Cymbidium lowianum

This is an extremely handsome species from Burma which produces long, arching sprays of beautiful, apple green flowers. When first introduced into Britain in 1878 it was considered to be a variety of *Cymbidium giganteum*, but later described as a separate species. There were at that time several named varieties, the most famous of which is *C. lowianum* var. *concolor*. In this variety the red blotch on the lip is replaced by orange yellow. The plant is a vigorous grower, producing large pseudo bulbs. The spikes are many flowered and bloom from March to May in Gt. Britain depending upon the clone. To this day plants of *C. lowianum* can be seen in bloom at the world famous Chelsea Flower Show.

Plants from the wild have not been exported from their native Burma for many years. The continuing demand for this orchid is being met by nursery raised plants produced from seed using selected varieties. Fortunately, while this orchid remains a firm favourite of amateur growers, nurserymen will continue to raise plants and maintain the numbers which are declining in the wild.

Very few green hybrids grown today cannot trace their pedigree back to either *C. lowianum* or *C. giganteum*, while many will have both species represented somewhere in their makeup. For its grace and beauty this splendid orchid will never be outshone by the more spectacular hybrids which it helped so frequently to produce.

Cymbidium Baldoyle 'Melbury'

This very beautiful hybrid is the result of crossing the white C. Balkis with an excellent deep pink C. Mission Bay. The latter is an American hybrid which has been used very successfully on both sides of the Atlantic to further the breeding of both standard and miniature Cymbidiums. C. Baydoyle was raised in 1962 by Dorset Orchids Ltd., England. While it was one of their finest hybrids, it was not destined to become as well known as some other hybrids from Balkis. Although it has not, to date, received any RHS awards, it is nevertheless a most outstanding Cymbidium which is certainly of award standard. The delicate pink shading of its petals and sepals and the lovely open lip creates a most pleasing combination of pastel shades to be found in any Cymbidium. This plant has been cultivated for many years as a top cut flower variety and is highly prized for its soft pastel colouring.

It flowers during the spring months of the year, and is an exceptionally robust grower. It will grow equally well when potted up for indoor or greenhouse culture, or set into a Cymbidium bed where it will grow rapidly into a large specimen plant.

Cymbidium Jolity 'Golden Heritage'

This is a delightful hybrid and an ideal plant for the amateur grower. The blooms are comparatively small and produced on a compact, upright flower spike. It flowers easily, very early in the *Cymbidium* season, and although the flowers are lacking in size it is not a true miniature as we have come to know them. Its modestly sized blooms makes it very popular as a cut flower *Cymbidium*, compensating for its lack of top quality texture.

Cymbidium Jolity was raised by Stewarts Inc., of Los Angeles in 1957, from two excellent parents, *C*. Eagle and *C*. Hanburyanum. Of these *C*. Eagle was raised from a very famous *C. eburneum* hybrid, *C*. Alexanderi 'Westonbirt' which was awarded an FCC by the Royal Horticultural Society in 1922. From that time it dominated the breeding of white *Cymbidiums* for many years. In the make up of its parents can be found several species, all of which have contributed in some way to *C*. Jolity. The most predominant contribution comes from *C. insigne*, a pink coloured species, extremely rare today. This species was at one time very popular in cultivation, and was used extensively in the early days of hybridising. From *C. insigne* comes the compact, upright habit which is the most notable characteristic. *C. lowianum* is one species which has been almost completely obscured, but may have contributed towards the delicate yellow colouring of the flowers. *C. tracyanum* has given to the plant its early flowering habit, while the influence of *C. erythrostylum* can be seen very slightly in the formation of the two lateral petals, which stand well up in the species. Very little influence has been retained from *C. eburneum*, present in both parents.

The flower spike produced by this plant has a soft stem and if left untied may be unable to support its weight of flowers, resulting in the spike snapping. To prevent this the spike should be tied to a supporting bamboo cane from an early age and allowed to grow upright. The ties should no be so tight as to interfere with the natural growth of the spike, and this spike should be kept straight. Unusual among the *Cymbidium* hybrids is the delicate perfume of the blooms. Several spikes can be produced in a season.

Cymbidium Balkis 'Solent Queen' FCC

This exceptionally fine hybrid is a typical example of a pure white *Cymbidium*. The cross was raised by Lional de Rothschild in his famous orchid greenhouses at Exbury, Gt. Britain, in 1934. Since that time it has remained as one of the top white *Cymbidiums* to be found in the world. The cross has been remade several times and there are many very fine varieties of Balkis, which have been acclaimed and awarded by orchidists all over the world. Balkis 'Solent Queen' received its FCC in 1956. This and many other varieties are widely available, and proven meristems or unflowered seedlings can be obtained.

The cross which produced *C.* Balkis was the result of combining *C.* Alexanderi 'Westonbirt' FCC and Rosanna 'Pinkie' FCC itself a child from Alexanderii 'Westonbirt'. This back crossing often proves successful in *Cymbidiums*, particularly with this hybrid. *C.* Balkis has not only proved to be an excellent hybrid, it has also in turn become an excellent parent plant, and from Balkis have come many more equally fine hybrids extending the line of white breeding even further. *Cymbidium* Balkis flowers during the middle of the *Cymbidium* season and is in great demand from florists who prize the clear white colouring and solid texture of the flowers which enables this *Cymbidium* to last in perfection for may weeks, as well as being a consistent winner of show bench awards.

When cutting flower spikes for use indoors it is always advisable to remove the whole spike from the plant when the last bud has opened and become fully set, usually in about a week to ten days. A sharp pruning knife which has been sterilised beforehand is best for this purpose, cutting through the stem of the spike close to the base of the bulb. For appearance any dried sheaths remaining on the stem can be removed. Sterilising the knife before use is advisable to minimise the danger of spreading virus disease from one plant to another. The easiest method is to pass the knife through a flame from a cigarette lighter.

Cymbidium San Francisco 'Mona Lisa' AM

This wonderful hybrid was raised by Stewarts Inc. of Los Angeles and registered by them in 1956. The parents of the cross are Blue Smoke, a very famous green flowered *Cymbidium* tracing back over many generations to *C. lowianum*, and used extensively for breeding through the green and yellow coloured varieties. The other parent being once again, the famous Balkis. Comparing San Francisco 'Mona Lisa' with the hybrid, Baldoyle, page 35, shows clearly the different colours which can be achieved by using one white parent with a *Cymbidium* of different colour. As can be seen in these two *Cymbidiums*, this influence produces pastel shades.

Since 1956 only two varieties of San Francisco have been awarded by the Royal Horticultural Society. The first of these was San Francisco 'Meadow Mist' AM, a beautiful sea green, suffused with pale pink. *C.* San Francisco 'Mona Lisa' exhibited by Burnham Nurseries Ltd., of Devon received its award in 1978 which makes it the most recently awarded *Cymbidium* in this book. There are many other very fine varieties of San Francisco, all of which are different from each other. Their colour range extends from white blushed pink, San Francisco 'Cynosure', to the delicate clear green of San Francisco 'Golden Gate' and the most delicate pink of San Francisco 'Powder Puff'.

Awards from the Royal Horticultural Society to *Cymbidiums* have dropped dramatically in the last decade due largely to the influence of meristemming. Fewer new *Cymbidiums* are being bred while the top favourites of recent years are being propagated by meristem. It may also be possible that certain lines of breeding have reached their ultimate in perfection. In earlier years the Royal Horticultural Society was being shown far more plants resulting in a large number of awards being given. Today there are fewer plants being submitted. Therefore it is even more unusual for a *Cymbidium* which is over twenty years old to receive an award as has happened with this hybrid.

Cymbidium Tapestry 'Long Beach'

This is one of the finest red *Cymbidiums* of all time, and certainly one of the finest *Cymbidiums* to come from the U.S.A. It was raised in 1963 by Rod McLellan & Co., of San Francisco. Its parents are *C.* Khyber Pass and *C.* Voodoo. Although these two *Cymbidiums* are not so well known as other red *Cymbidiums*, their progeny Tapestry has become extremely famous and acclaimed throughout the world as a *Cymbidium* of exceptional merit. Among its many attributes are its rich powerful colouring and shapely habit. The flowers hold their shape extremely well, unlike many of the red *Cymbidiums* whose petals twist and curl as the flowers mature.

Tapestry 'Long Beach' has not proved to be a very successful parent, and appears to be the end of this particular line of breeding for the present. However, on its own merit it will remain among the top reds for many years to come. It is not difficult to see that this type of *Cymbidium* has come a very long way from the original species, and while it can be traced back to *C. insigne* and *C. lowianum*, their influence has become obscured through the generations of selected breeding. Two famous parents stand out from this plant's pedigree, these being Ceres 'F. J. Hanbury' FCC/RHS and Rio Rita, both have contributed to the rich colouring and quality of Tapestry 'Long Beach'. Both the parents of Tapestry 'Long Beach' show strong Ceres characteristics.

Cymbidium Ormoulu

For its solid golden colour this is one of the finest *Cymbidiums* in cultivation today. The superb quality and colour of the flower, which does not tone as the flower matures, is the result of crossing two famous *Cymbidiums*, *C*. Pearl Beryl and *C*. Baltic. This British cross was made by Baron Schroder in 1957. The plant can be traced back through many generations to the species where *C. lowianum* is found to be predominant. Two outstanding hybrids involved with its breeding are again, the pink *C*. Pauwelsii, with many flowers on an arching spike, and *C*. Pearl 'Magnificium', in its time an exceptionally fine yellow *Cymbidium*, awarded an FCC by the Royal Horticultural Society, and noted for its long arching sprays with many flowers. While these once famous plants are no longer grown to any extent, the beautiful hybrids such as *C*. Ormoulu have surpassed them and now hold pride of place in their own right.

The beautifully red blotched lip which is such a startling feature of *C*. Ormoulu comes through from the parent *C*. Baltic. This awarded *Cymbidium* is a deep apple green, with the contrasting red blotched lip which has been so successfully reproduced in Ormoulu.

Cymbidium Vieux Rose 'Del Park' FCC

This plant is very famous both as a hybrid of great beauty and as a breeder of equally fine hybrids. The parents, *C.* Babylon and *C.* Rio Rita are also both well known and famous in their own right. The cross was made and registered by Lord Hothfield in 1949 and many fine plants were selected from it for future breeding. This particular variety showing Babylon influence was exhibited by Baron Schroder when it received its FCC in 1953. From that time Vieux Rose became as successful as its famous parents. From the *C.* Babylon comes the very round lip which was to become a most desirable feature of the pink coloured *Cymbidiums* and which was carried successfully through Vieux Rose and on to future breeding. The short, upright spikes which is a characteristic of this hybrid make it an ideal cut flower variety. The florists often prefer short flower spikes with just a few large flowers. It is a mid season *Cymbidium* and flowers freely with ease. Raised and bred in Britain it now enjoys equal popularity on both sides of the Atlantic.

When this picture was taken the flower spike had been in bloom for over eight weeks. The plant had been exhibited at more than one major flower show and had travelled several hundreds of miles. How well the blooms have stood up to this perambulating can clearly be seen. Apart from a slight reflexing of the petals at their edges the flowers have kept extremely well and the colour has retained its freshness.

While Vieux Rose is considered a typical pink flowered *Cymbidium*, its colour is overlaid by a fine network of lines running through the petals. Compare this hybrid with the Baldoyle 'Melbury' which in contrast is a self coloured shell pink. Both hybrids would be classified as pink and they illustrate the great variation to be found in just one colour of the range among *Cymbidiums*.

Cymbidium Featherhill 'Heritage' AM

The excellent substance and conformation of this wonderfully coloured *Cymbidium* have made it highly successful the world over. It has received awards in Gt. Britain, the U.S.A. and South Africa. It has been produced along another line of *C.* Babylon breeding, using *C.* Spartan Queen which has helped to give the darker colour to the flowers. There are several excellent varieties of Featherhill, all of which were produced in the U.S.A. One further variety of note is Featherhill 'Amazon', which is a beautiful rosy pink flower. This plant is exceptional for producing many spikes each with up to 20 flowers. Featherhill 'Heritage' also carries many flowers on a spike, and both of these exceptional plants were raised by Eliot Haberlitz in 1956. *C.* Featherhill 'Heritage' has made its mark not only as a cut flower *Cymbidium*, but also as a fine choice for the amateur's collection.

These darker shades are more popular on the continent of Europe where they are often preferred to the pastel shades so loved in Britain. Many of these dark rich pinks should be kept well shaded when the buds start to open, particularly if they are flowering late in the season when the sun is much stronger. Otherwise they are likely to fade to a dull slate grey and become prematurely spotted. Shading will help the flowers to last longer in perfection.

Cymbidiums which produce full, heavy spikes are better if the flowers can be cut as soon as possible after opening, especially if the plant is blooming late in the season and the new growth is already showing. If the plant is in need of repotting the earlier this can be done after flowering the better it is for the plant.

Cymbidium Mimi 'Aconague'

This is an excellent example of a first generation miniature *Cymbidium* hybrid raised from the species *C. pumilum* and the standard *C.* Doris Aurea. The species *C. pumilum* originates from Japan and Formosa and is a true miniature which produces very small flowers on a spike a mere 6 in. (15 cm) high. The individual blooms are petite, and the type is coloured reddish brown. There is also a well known albino variety, *C. pumilum* var. *album*, with greeny yellow flowers. Although not a very important or showy species in its own right, it has tremendous potential and has become a most important species in the breeding of miniature *Cymbidiums*. The most impressive hybrids are always the first generation crosses, where the size of the standard *Cymbidium* is reduced to about half. When these first generation hybrids are bred on it becomes increasingly difficult to maintain the small size of plant and flowers, and by the second or third generation the plants have very often reverted to standard size.

The true worth of the miniature *Cymbidium* is that they can be accomodated in pots under 6 in. (15 cm) and are more manageable than the standards. While their culture remains the same, they are undoubtedly easier to cope with in limited surroundings.

Cymbidium Mimi shows much *C. pumilum* influence in the lip and shape of the flowers. The *C.* Doris Aurea is a standard hybrid bred along conventional lines, but is unusual, for being a champagne straw colour, always passes on to its progeny the rich red colouring to be seen in *C.* Mimi. It is an American hybrid, and was raised by Greenoaks in 1961, since when it has become a top selling miniature on both sides of the Atlantic.

Cymbidium Jill 'Katalinca'

Here is one further striking example of a first generation hybrid using *C. pumilum* as the miniature parent, this time crossing with the standard *C.* Miretta, a very famous green renowned for its excellent colouring and good round shape. In *C.* Jill it can be readily seen that the Miretta has influenced the colour wholly, while the shape and colouring of the lip is remarkably similar to Mimi. This shows consistent influence from *C. pumilum* over its progeny. This excellent miniature was raised in U.S.A. in 1964 by Ireland.

These miniature *Cymbidiums* have set the standard for their types and this particular line of breeding is producing an alternative size of bloom which is becoming increasingly popular with the florists, many of whom prefer the smaller blooms.

Little or no breeding has been done with these two *Cymbidiums*, and further hybrids produced from them will either increase the size of the bloom when they will become merged with the standards, or if taken back to the miniature parent, *C. pumilum*, would produce nothing of better value. This beautiful miniature is a consistent pre-Christmas bloomer.

Cymbidium Cariad 'Plush'

This charming little hybrid represents a novelty line of breeding in *Cymbidiums*. Here the flower cannot be judged for shape or size, or even cut flower ability. But is something quite different for the hobbyist and we feel sure it has a tremendous future with the amateur grower. The plant is a small, compact grower, ideal where space is limited, and produces a semi pendent flower spike, with many flowers, and often several spikes on a mature plant.

The breeding behind this delightful miniature is two species, *C. elegans* and *C. devonianum*. *C. elegans* is a species from India which blooms early in the season. It produces long sprays of elegant, bell shaped fragrant flowers, very compact on the spike. The sepals and petals are narrow, coloured corn yellow, while the lip is lightly marked. The elongated pseudo bulbs carry an abundance of foliage. The influence of *C. elegans* can clearly be seen in the shape of the petals and lip of *C.* Cariad. *C. devonianum* which is another miniature from India can clearly be seen in the dark colouring on the lip, a characteristic so often carried through in its offspring. This plant has diminutive pseudo bulbs and broad leaves. The flower spike emerges horizontally from the base of the bulb and assumes a pendent habit. The spike is many flowered, with small, closely set blooms. These vary considerably in colour, but the type is olive green, the petals and sepals lined with reddish brown. The small lip is coloured with rich purple, a feature which comes through strongly.

C. Cariad is strictly a bigeneric cross, while *Cymbidium elegans* has been known and recorded under this name for many years, it is now correctly known as *Cyperorchis elegans*. However, this botanical error was corrected only after it had been bred from as *Cymbidium*, and therefore this name has been accepted by the registrar of orchid hybrids, and the correct bigeneric genus of *Cypercymbidium* is not generally recognised.

C. Cariad 'Plush' illustrates an exciting and fresh outlook on miniature *Cymbidium* breeding, and while it does not attract the attention of the awards committee, it is nevertheless a modern concept in miniature *Cymbidiums*. This charming little plant was raised in Britain by Keith Andrew Orchids Ltd., of Plush.

Cymbidium Bulbarrow 'Friar Tuck' AM

While in the U.S.A. *C. pumilum* has become the most important miniature species used for breeding, in Britain more concentration has been placed on *C. devonianum*. *C.* Bulbarrow is a fine example of first generation breeding crossing *C. devonianum* with a top quality standard *Cymbidium*. In this case, *C.* Western Rose, a product of the famous *C.* Alexanderi 'Westonbirt' FCC and *C.* Vieux Rose. The former is an exceptionally fine pink *Cymbidium* and seemed an excellent choice to cross with *C. devonianum*. This assumption has asserted itself in the perfect shape and substance of *C.* Bulbarrow, making this particular awarded variety the most perfectly shaped hybrid from *C. devonianum* to date. The influence of *C. devonianum* may not be so predominant as usual, but has given to *C.* Bulbarrow the most pleasing colour of the sepals and petals as well as the striking lip markings. This very fine modern hybrid was registered in 1976 having been raised in Gt. Britain by Keith Andrew Orchids Ltd., at Plush.

'Friar Tuck' is not the only Bulbarrow to have received an RHS award. Several awards have come from this excellent cross including Bulbarrow 'Will Stutely' AM/RHS 1978 and these were quickly followed by American awards when they were seen in the United States.

The flower spike illustrated has been purposely trained upright. With the strong influence of *C. devonianum* many of these hybrids can look equally attractive when left to hang over the rim of the pot as they will do naturally. When the plant is suspended with the flowers at eye level their beauty can be fully enjoyed away from the foliage. However, one should be careful when watering hanging plants that the flowers do not get wet.

All the first generation hybrids from *C. devonianum* have a distinctive appearance. From their species parent they inherit to an extent the broad, dark green leaves and small, rounded pseudo bulbs which make them instantly recognizable when not in bloom.

Odontoglossum harryanum

This very beautiful *Odontoglossum* species was discovered in 1886, when it was hailed as one of the most handsome *Odontoglossums* ever discovered. It is an extremely variable species and also known under the synonym of *O. wyattianum*, or *O. harryanum* var. *wyattianum*. The plant produces large pseudo bulbs with a pair of broad leaves. The flower spikes may be about the same height as the foliage, or rise to over a foot (30 cm) above. Depending upon the variety it may carry six to eight blooms, or up to a dozen on a taller spike. The shorter flowered variety is usually fragrant. Its flowering period can also vary, although generally autumn flowering. It is still possible to import plants of *O. harryanum*, and while the original importations came from Colombia, good specimens are obtained from Peru.

In the early years of hybridising *Odontoglossum harryanum* was crossed with just about every other *Odontoglossum* species, and later it was crossed with hybrids and other genera from the *Odontoglossum* alliance. The plant proved very worth while as a parent, contributing much colour to its progeny. The strong lip markings in particular were a predominant feature of those early hybrids, an attribute which has been successfully carried through more than one generation of hybrids. *O. harryanum* is also responsible for creating many of the yellow *Odontoglossums*, and its influence remains in many of the present day hybrids.

Odontoglossum rossii

This *Odontoglossum* is a small, compact growing species which comes from Mexico and Guatemala. It was introduced into Gt. Britain in 1842 since when it has been consistently popular. It is a highly variable species, of which there are a few named varieties. Of these, *O. rossii* var. *majus* and *O. rossii* var. *rubescens* can be obtained today. The photograph shows two different and typical clones of the type. It can be seen that the one form has a pure white lip and column, while the other has a pink flushed lip with a purple column. In the variety *majus* the flowers are much larger than the type and may be slightly suffused with pink on the lip. The variety *rubescens* contains much pink flushing, particularly on the lip, and the flowers are smaller than the type.

Odontoglossum rossii is a species which is ideal for the amateur grower with limited space, particularly for the beginner who can be assured the plant is easy to grow and free flowering. It also makes an ideal subject to be grown on cork bark, as an alternative to pot culture.

At one time *O. rossii* was used extensively to cross with other *odontoglossum* species and again with a variety of the early hybrids. Due to its small size and the desire at that time for larger, well rounded flowers, it lost favour as a parent. Today, however, with an increasing demand for novelty type flowers in all genera, *O. rossii* is once again being used as a parent, and producing some very exciting and colourful hybrids. With their modest size, these have created much interest at home and abroad.

The plant is seen at its best when it has been grown on for a number of years without division. Even the largest plants can be easily contained in pans when they may be suspended in the roof of the greenhouse. This was a favourite method of culture used in victorian times when the blooms would cascade freely over the rim of the pot.

Odontoglossum bictoniense

Another commanding *Odontoglossum* species well suited to the beginner. The plant is of average size, although large specimen plants can become considerably bigger. The leaves are narrow and the plant will produce each new bulb slightly above the previous one, so that it is growing continually upward. It produces an abundant root system, the roots being considerably thick for the genus.

It was imported to Gt. Britain from Guatemala in 1835, but did not gain tremendous popularity and was considered at that time to be less important than others of the genus. Today however, it enjoys immense popularity because it can be grown and flowered with great ease in a variety of surroundings. The illustration shows a portion of a very long flower spike. This can be tall and upright, the many flowers usually facing the same way. A well grown plant can produce two or even three large, often branched spikes from a single bulb. The flowering period commences during the latter part of the summer, when the season's pseudo bulb is partially completed. The flowers last a very long time in perfection, and exceptionally fine plants are a regular feature at the orchid shows throughout the autumn. The illustration shows a typical flower although there is a great variation between the different clones. Several named varieties were originally described although it is difficult to distinguish these from the many different coloured forms available today. The lip can vary from pure white to deep rosy pink, while the petals and sepals which are more usually light green barred with brown, can vary from pale yellow with no markings, to almost complete covering with heavy brown marking.

To the early hybridisers it was not considered to be of much importance, but in latter years some extremely beautiful first generation hybrids have been seen from *O. bictoniense*, particularly on the continent of Europe where the highly coloured hybrids are acclaimed as very desirable house plants.

Odontoglossum pulchellum

A truly delightful species, modest in size and easy to grow and flower in profusion. The plant produces slender pseudo bulbs with a pair of slim leaves. The flower spike appears in the spring producing up to ten modestly sized flowers. These are startling white, with a deep yellow blotch on the crest of the lip. The flowers are held with the lip uppermost, an unusual feature among *Odontoglossums*. The plant has always been distinct and is now correctly an *Osmoglossum*, a smaller genus to which it was recently moved although for horticultural purposes, it is still classified as an *Odontoglossum*. It is at its best when grown on into a large specimen plant, when its beauty can be enjoyed to the full.

The species was introduced into Britain from its native Guatemala in 1840, where it won immediate fame for its ease of culture, and the wonderful fragrance of its petite flowers.

Among this species, there is virtually no variation and there is only one recorded variety. This is *O. pulchellum* var. *egertoni*, a smaller form of the type, the flowers not opening fully. No breeding of any note has been achieved with *Odontoglossum pulchellum*, which as a species is a distinct and desirable addition to any collection. Possibly hybridising has nothing to add to this already, completely charming species.

During the winter a semi dry rest is required, giving just enough water to the plant to prevent shrivelling. The back bulbs will remain on the plant in a green leafless state for many years and should be removed when they outnumber the leaved bulbs. In cultivation the whole plant can become very yellow if insufficient feed is given. It is therefore advisable to give a little extra artificial feed while the plant is in its growing season.

Oncidium tigrinum

Here is a most showy species which produces very large, branching sprays of beautifully fragrant flowers. When introduced from Mexico in 1840 it gained instant recognition as a most handsome plant well worthy of a place in the best collections. It is a strong, robust grower and has an equally impressive variety, *unquiculatum.* In the latter the plant is more robust and can become as large as a *Cymbidium.* The many flowered, branching spikes can be over six feet (2 metres) tall. The individual flowers are smaller than the type with more yellow about the petals and sepals. The lip differs slightly in shape and is coloured a slightly paler shade of yellow. Both varieties have been grown, especially in Europe, as cut flower orchids, where their delicate type of blooms are greatly admired. The photograph shows the type and illustrates a single branch from the large flowering spike, enabling the reader to see the fine colouring of the flower in detail.

Oncidium tigrinum was originally crossed with other popular *Oncidium* species and produced nothing very startling. In latter years it began to be used in conjunction with *Odontoglossums* and other genera among the alliance. Many of the results were breathtaking. The hybrids carried the rich yellow colouring of *tigrinum*, and the lip especially carried not only the clear colouring but also the large size and in some the fragrance was carried on to greater enhance the hybrids. Today, due entirely to the influence of *Oncidium tigrinum* there is a wonderful range of intergeneric hybrids from it. While there is a dominance of yellow and brown, some pink and red flowered hybrids are being flowered when *O. tigrinum* has been crossed with predominantly dark flowered *Odontoglossums.* It is most gratifying that while this beautiful species is still plentiful today we may also enjoy a wide variety of beautiful hybrids from it.

Odontoglossum cordatum

This is an extremely pretty species which is among the most popular of the *Odontoglossum* species. The plant has light green bulbs and foliage and produces a number of aerial roots. It has a short resting period and blooms from the completed bulb during the late spring and early summer. It is a native of Guatemala and Mexico and was introduced into Europe in 1837. It is an extremely variable species of which there are one or two named varieties. These varieties were described many years ago from clones imported at that time. It is difficult with the plants in cultivation today to distinguish these named varieties from a batch, where each clone varies slightly from the next. The plant illustrated can be considered a fine example of the species with excellent colouring, and a good sized bloom. Some varieties are much paler, including *O. cordatum* var. *sulphureum*, which is pure sulphur yellow and devoid of the brown markings. This very distinct variety is seldom seen today.

Odontoglossum cordatum is similar to another species. *O. maculatum* which combines similar colours with a slightly smaller flower. Out of flower the two plants are difficult to tell apart.

The blooms of *Odontoglossum cordatum* can be cut and placed in water when they will last for several weeks. The plant has never been used for hybridising to any extent and recently very limited hybrids have appeared where *O. cordatum* has been crossed with other related genera.

Miltonia Emotion

This is a fine example of the typical *Miltonia* hybrid. These beautiful orchids are very popular in cultivation and grown extensively in Europe as house plants. The flowers are round and flat, and the large distinguishing lip has earned *Miltonias* the common name of 'Pansy Orchid'. The type illustrated here has been raised from the soft leaved Columbian species, such as *Miltonia vexillaria* and *roezelii*. Both these delightful, and now rare species had many different coloured forms, and with selective breeding it has been possible to produce many hybrids in a whole range of colours, from pure white, through cream, yellow and pink to the exceptionally dark reds. These darker colours have the sheen of velvet which is unique to *Miltonias* and through them has been bred into other related genera with superb results.

Miltonias are very free flowering orchids, often producing two spikes of up to six blooms on each. While they will remain on the plant for many weeks, they do not last when cut, and are therefore not grown for that purpose.

Miltonia Emotion is a French bred hybrid, raised by Vacherot & Lecoufle in 1962. Its parents are Emio and Nyasa, both exceptionally fine hybrids.

Odontoglossum Opheron, **crispum** and Hyrastro

Our first picture in this section shows three typical, pure bred *Odontoglossum* hybrids of which there are several thousand available today. These hybrids have been bred through many generations of line breeding to produce tall sprays of very showy blooms. The top hybrid is *O*. Opheron raised in 1952 by the well known British firm of Charlesworth & Co. It is a plant which has in turn been greatly hybridised from and is noted for its gracefully arching spike and well spaced flowers. The bottom hybrid is a plant of *O*. Hyrastro, a very modern hybrid raised in 1966, again by Charlesworth & Co. The plant has been raised along similar lines to *O*. Opheron, but shows some differences, particularly in this shorter, upright flower spike, with the blooms set more closely together. These are larger and have a more rounded shape, which are the qualities continually looked for in the perfect exhibition bloom. It can also be seen that both these hybrids hold their shape extremely well. Although the *O*. Hyrastro tends to fold its lower sepals. While these two varieties undoubtedly contain some *O. crispum* in their pedigree, stronger coloured varieties have been responsible for achieving the high colouring. The centre *Odontoglossum* illustrates a very fine variety of *O. crispum*. This thoroughbred is the result of selective breeding from individual varieties of the species, *O. crispum*. It is a Colombian species and was introduced into Britain in 1841, when it was found to be highly variable. The finest clones were given varietal names and selected for line breeding to improve the shape and texture of the blooms. While many of the original plants of *O. crispum* were coloured forms, the pure white varieties were used to produce the modern day *O. crispum* hybrids, which may be pure white, or slightly suffused with pink. Some show the occasional blotching on the petals and sepals which is another variation and not considered in any way a fault. The illustrated *O. crispum* is a young plant with a small flower spike of three blooms. The quality is outstanding, and as the plant becomes older and stronger it will produce a full spike of up to a dozen fine flowers.

Odontioda Minel 'Oregon'

The *Odontioda* is a bigeneric cross between *Cochlioda* and *Odontoglossum*. It was one of the first bigeneric hybrids to be produced, and the original cross was made by using the small, brightly coloured species, *Cochlioda noezliana* with *Odontoglossum pescatorie*, a prettily marked species, both very rare today. The cross produced *Odontioda* Vuylstekeae and was registered in 1904. Since that time many thousands of *Odontioda* hybrids have been made, until today they have become merged with the *Odontoglossums* to such an extent that it is difficult to tell them apart. The *Odontioda* Minel illustrated clearly shows the very rich colouring which has been inherited from the *Cochlioda noezliana* and which made the earliest *Odontiodas* so distinct from the more delicately coloured *Odontoglossums*.

Odontioda Minel 'Oregon' is a British raised hybrid, produced by Charlesworth & Co., in 1965. Its parents were Elpheon and Minosha. The exceptionally rich colouring and tall arching habit of the spike has made this a highly desirable hybrid in the U.S.A. as well as Britain. However, the slight pinching visible on the lower petals make it highly unlikely that this plant will ever receive an award. Although its shape is not perfect, this does not affect its cut flower ability for which it is excellent. Minel 'Oregon' is superior to most others of the cross owing to its solid red colouring which is unbroken in the petals and sepals. Most other Minels show more intricate patterning of red on a white ground. The long arching spike illustrated can only be expected from a fully mature plant. Younger plants which have not yet reached their maximum potential will only give seven or eight blooms.

Odontioda Hambühren

This hybrid represents a renewed modern day interest in breeding primary hybrids from the species, *Odontoglossum rossii*. This species was at one time used considerably in the production of early hybrids, but lost favour through its smaller size. The demand was for ever increasing large, round flowers. Now that these are so plentiful the trend is to return to the species where great charm can be found in the first generation crosses, as *O.* Hambühren clearly shows.

The influence of *O. rossii* can be seen in the shape and the quantity of flowers while the other parent, *O.* Feurerschein has contributed to the fine, rich colouring. Whenever *O. rossii* is used for breeding, small compact plants with highly coloured flowers are the result. Their popularity with the small greenhouse owner is understandable, and is causing nurserymen to raise many more. This hybrid will therefore surely be the forerunner of new breeding lines which are being carried out at the famous German nursery of Artur Elle & Co. Hybrids from *O. rossii* will always have fewer blooms to a spike but this is more than made up for by their colourful and fresh appearance.

The rich colouring has been achieved by using a dark flowered *Odontioda*. It will be interesting to see if hybrids of different colours can be achieved in the future while retaining the same brightness. One may imagine *O. rossii* crossed with some of the outstanding hybrids from *Oncidium tigrinum* could give the most stunning of yellows! At the time of writing these modern hybrids are still so new their full potential is still to be realised and so far none are being offered as meristemmed plants. However, this should change within the next few years.

Odontonia Debutante 'Oxbow'

This exciting hybrid is the result of an unusual type of breeding. It is a bigeneric hybrid between an *Odontoglossum* and *Miltonia*. *O. cariniferum* is a species not often seen in hybridising which produces large, well marked flowers on a stout, branched flower spike. The flowers are olive brown tipped with yellow. It arrived from Central America in 1848 but has not been grown extensively for many years. *Miltonia warscewiczii* is totally unlike the previously described 'Pansy orchids'. It is a hard leaved species from Peru and differs from most *Miltonias* in its many flowered, branching flower spikes. The flowers are strikingly coloured with rich rose purple. The lip is also extraordinary in its shape and peculiar 'window' in the form of a yellowish blotch. This strange feature is carried through to its progeny and can be seen as a pinkish bar on the upper portion of the lip of Debutante. This beautiful, first generation *Odontonia* is not typical of the genus, but is a most exciting hybrid of great distinction.

Odontonia Debutante 'Oxbow' is a large, robust growing plant, with the vigour obtained from both its parents. It will produce two very large, branching flower spikes from one bulb which will last for a long time in perfection. It is an American raised hybrid, registered in 1960 and awarded the AM by the American Orchid Society.

At the present time there are very few other hybrids available from either of the two species used in this cross. Debutante will undoubtedly remain a very popular plant for many years to come. Fortunately, the plant propagates readily by the conventional methods of division and back bulbs as well as lending itself to meristemming.

Although the individual blooms are small for corsage work, the complete sprays last long in water and are ideal for table decoration.

Odontonia Sappho 'Excul'

This beautiful hybrid is more typical of conventional *Odontonia* breeding. It is the result of crossing the soft leaved Columbian *Miltonia* with an *Odontoglossum* hybrid. The result is the very beautiful *Odontonia* which shows clearly the *Miltonia* influence in the large size, and soft colouring. These *Odontonia* hybrids produce large flower spikes, the individual flowers are equal in size to the *Miltonia*. This *Odontonia* is a very old hybrid raised in 1925 by Charlesworth & Co., in Britain. The parents were *Odontoglossum* Aphrodite and *Miltonia* Charlesworthii. At the time when this hybrid was raised, it was an individual, and once passed into a private collection could easily have become lost with the passage of time. However, being so outstanding it was carefully retained until the technique of meristemming made it available in unlimited numbers. Now, this is one more beautiful hybrid which enjoys a popularity unthought of in its youth.

While this and the previous *Odontonia* are both on the same generic line of breeding, the species represented are both totally different and the hybrids therefore bear no resemblance to each other, but show clearly the different extremes which can be obtained. Here *Miltonia vexillaria* is dominant, and this hybrid can be compared with the *Miltonia* Emotion mentioned earlier.

From the cultural point of view both *Odontonias* can be grown alongside each other in the company of the *Odontoglossums* and under the same conditions.

Odontocidium Crowborough 'Plush'

This is an extremely pretty, first generation hybrid between *Odontoglossum* Golden Guinea which is a top quality hybrid, of exceptionaloy fine yellow colouring, and the species *Oncidium leucochilum*. The latter is a South American variety which is extremely popular among amateur growers. It is fragrant, and carries an extremely tall spike which can exceed 6 ft (2 m.) with a gracefully arching habit. The flowers, produced on short branches are star shaped, the petals and sepals olive green and barred with red brown, and white lip. It is a elegant and variable species from which *Odontocidium* Crowborough has inherited the fine colouring and shape. While the *Odontoglossum* Golden Guinea has contributed the deep yellow in the petals and sepals. *Odontocidium* Crowborough lasts for many weeks in perfection and blooms mainly during the spring months. The illustration shows the top portion of a very long branching spike to show clearly the fine details of the flower.

These flower spikes emerge from the base of the bulb and at first appear very dark, almost black. One could be forgiven for mistaking this for a diseased growth but it is not an unnatural colouration. The flower spikes grow at a tremendous rate and will later require some support in the form of a bamboo cane tied to the base of the buds. The spike can then be trained in an arching or circular shape, the advantage of training these spikes into hoops is that less headroom is required.

This hybrid was raised by Stuart Low & Co., in England, and they used the grex name Crowborough on several occasions for the plants they produced. *Odontocidium* Crowborough should not be confused with *Oncidioda* Crowborough mentioned later in this book.

Odontocidium Tigersun

This is a further *Odontocidium* hybrid, again a primary cross, this time using *Oncidium tigrinum* as a parent. This species has been used very successfully many times for this type of bigeneric breeding. *Odontoglossum* Sunmar is a very fine yellow flowered variety, which has become a successful parent with *Odontoglossum* and intergeneric breeding. *Odontocidium* Tigersun has proved to be consistently good, and is in great demand in the U.S.A. and Britain where it was raised by Mansell & Hatcher in 1977.

The flowers have great appeal for their bright colouring, which retains its brightness as the flower matures. The bold, chestnut patterning is typical of the cross, and the flower is set off by the large, frilled lip which is the main contribution from the species. The plant is of typical *Odontoglossum* size and has inherited the vigour of growth from the species, giving the plant a wide tolerance of varying conditions.

This line of breeding from *Oncidium tigrinum* shows great potential. The flowers hold their colour well, seldom fading and they also last well when placed in water. This makes them of particular importance to the cut flower grower many of whom are showing interest in these hybrids.

As parent plants we expect to see the next generation even more exciting. The breeding already done shows great promise. One outstanding example has been produced recently in the USA. This was a cross between *Odontocidium* Tiger Butter, another *Oncidium tigrinum* hybrid, and *Brassia verrucosa*. The resulting man-made genus is *Maclellanara*, named after the raisers, Rod McLellan & Co. Ltd.

Oncidioda Crowborough 'Chelsea' AM

This extraordinary hybrid is quite unique through its breeding. It is the result of two generations of crossing originating with *Oncidium macranthum*, which is an extremely beautiful plant and the largest to come from Ecuador. It belongs to a small group of very distinct *Oncidiums* which are less frequently known under the separate genus *Cyrtochilum*. It is a large, robust grower which produces a very tall spike capable of reaching up to 15 ft (4$\frac{1}{2}$ m.). The spike is branched along its length, each branch carrying several large, bright yellow flowers. There are no flowers on the main stem which can be trained in a hoop to contain it in a small space. When this, now unobtainable species, was crossed with the small and petite *Cochlioda noetzliana*, of *Odontioda* fame, it produced *Oncidioda* Cooksoniae, and this was made as early as 1912 by Charlesworth & Co. In 1950 *Oncidioda* Crowborough was registered, the cross having been made by Stuart Low & Co., of Britain, between *O.* Cooksoniae and *Oncidium auriferum*, a yellow flowered species from Venezuela. Through both generations the influence of *Oncidium macranthum* has come through very strongly to *Oncidioda* Crowborough. The plant is a large grower which produces the tremendously tall *Cochlioda noezliana*, of *Odontioda* fame, it produced *Oncidioda* Cooksoniae, and this was *Cochlioda noezliana* has contributed the unmistakable russet red.

In 1955 *Oncidioda* Crowborough was awarded an AM by the Royal Horticultural Society at the Chelsea Flower Show in May. Since then it has been meristemmed successfully.

Vuylstekeara Monica 'Burnham'

The *Vuylstekeara* is a multi generic hybrid, containing *Cochlioda, Miltonia* and *Odontoglossum* in its makeup. The genus was named after Mr. C. Vuylsteke from Ghent in Belgium who was the originator of this genus. The hybrids are all highly prized for their large, flamboyant flowers, which have inherited so many of the good qualities from their different parents. The plants are most often more robust, extremely easy to grow and exceptionally free flowering from a very early age. It is these qualities which have made the *Vuylstekearas* outstanding orchids among the *Odontoglossum* alliance.

Vuylstekeara Monica 'Burnham' has been chosen for its remarkably rich, self colouring. It was raised again by the famous firm of Charlesworth & Co., who dominated the breeding of hybrids within the *Odontoglossum* alliance for so many years. The parents of *V*. Monica are *Vuylstekeara* Aspasia and *Odontioda* Columbia and it was registered in 1932. Today, Monica is readily available having been selected for its superb colouring for propagation by meristemming.

Vuylstekeara Yokara 'Perfection'

One further outstanding example of the beautiful *Vuylstekearas*. This perfectly shaped hybrid is in complete contrast to the previous illustrations, and portrays more features from the *Odontoglossum*, and *Miltonia* blood being less dominant. The hybrid is a very strong grower and is capable of producing very long flower spikes on a mature plant. Its rich colourings and exceptional fine patterning has made this a very popular hybrid. It was raised by Charlesworth & Co., in 1938, when it was in advance of its time. Its parents were *Vuylstekeara* Leda and *Odontioda* Dorila. Both these hybrids were plants of fine quality which have nevertheless been surpassed by their offspring.

There was at one time a number of plants in existence known as *Vuylstekeara* Frederica 'Perfection'. However, this name was proved to be incorrect and the plants were identified as Yokara 'Perfection'. Even today a few mislabelled plants remain in collections. One feature of this orchid is the slow development of the flower spike and the gradual opening of the buds which can take many weeks. The first blooms may be past their prime before the final bud has opened.

Vuylstekeara Cambria 'Plush' FCC

It is no exaggeration to say that this is the most famous plant among the *Vuylstekearas* and indeed among the whole family of orchid hybrids. This supreme orchid has been a consistent award winner the world over, and is grown more profusely than any other of its type. Its beautifully formed flowers, combined with large size and rich contrasting colours gives it instant appeal. It is a plant grown by amateurs and cut flower specialists alike, and has been raised in its tens of thousands to meet the world wide demand since it was first meristemmed only a decade or so ago. As a parent it has proved disappointing, usually little seed is produced, and the few seedlings which have been successfully raised have been of little value, and do not come up to their famous parent.

    Vuylstekeara Cambria was raised by Charlesworth & Co., in 1931 its parents were *V.* Rudra and *O.* Clonius. With the change to modern culture, the plant grew even better, and was awarded the FCC by the Royal Horticultural Society when exhibited by Keith Andrew Orchids Ltd., in 1967. It pedigree can be traced back to the species *O. harryanum* which can still be seen in the spectacular lip, also *Miltonia vexillaria* and the unmistakable colouring of *Cochlioda noezliana*. Other species in the makeup of Cambria which have become lost through five generations are *O. crispum* and *O. pescatorie*.

Wilsonara Lyoth 'Ruby' AM

Three separate genera make the trigeneric genus *Wilsonara*. These are *Cochlioda, Odontoglossum* and *Oncidium*. By using these genera in many different combinations with a variety of plants many different *Wilsonaras* have been produced with greatly contrasting features.

Wilsonara Lyoth 'Ruby' is a hybrid from *Odontioda* Venusta which is an offspring of *Cochlioda noezliana*, and a little known *Oncidium* species, *O. claesianum*. This latter appears to have contributed little to its progeny which is completely dominated by the grandparent, *Cochlioda neozliana* and which has carried on the exciting red colour very clearly throughout the whole flower. The flowers themselves are somewhat small, again showing the *C. noetzliana* influence, but beautifully spaced on the stem, and their simple form and clear colouring makes it a very refreshing flower which can never fail to please.

The plant was raised by Charlesworth in 1947, and received an AM from the Royal Horticultural Society in the following year. It is still considered an exceptional plant today, and once a collectors item available in very limited numbers is now widely grown, due to propagation by meristemming.

Wilsonara Widecombe Fair

This enchanting *Wilsonara* shows great variation from the previous picture. While it contains the same genera as *Wilsonara* Lyoth, it has been bred from completely separate species with equally different results. It is a first generation hybrid from *Odontioda* Florence Stirling. This is a very famous *Odontioda*, of which there were many extremely good varieties all of which show rich purple colouring. It has been used extensively as a parent, and is contained in the makeup of many of the modern hybrids. The other parent is the species, *Oncidium incurvum*, which is a pink flowered variety from Mexico. It produces a tall, slender flower spike which branches freely and carries many pink and white flowers. The petals and sepals are narrow and the lip is small and neat. From this combination *Wilsonara* Widecombe Fair has emerged as a captivating hybrid. It carries the large, branching spike greatly influenced by the species, as also the flowers, which are modestly sized, but extremely attractive. The plant is typical *Odontoglossum* in size and as is found so often with these intergeneric hybrids grows and flowers exceedingly well. The plant blooms between January and March in the northern hemisphere and lasts for weeks in perfection. This hybrid was raised by Burnham Nurseries Ltd., in Britain and registered by them in 1973. Since when it has gained much favour in the U.S.A. as well as Britain and Europe.

Wilsonara Tigerwood

Another very charming modern *Wilsonara* hybrid, again illustrating the successful dominance of *Oncidium tigrinum*, which in this hybrid was used with *Odontioda* Doric. The flowers are neat and compact with the petals and lip of equal size. The strong, chocolate markings have come from both parents, while the large, bright yellow lip is typical of the influence from *Oncidium tigrinum*. The illustration shows a young seedling which is flowering for the first time and which shows great potential. On a mature plant the flowering spike will be much larger with three times as many flowers. The solid texture of the blooms has been achieved by using a top quality *Odontioda*, and this winning combination carries all the hallmarks of the award standard plant.

Oncidium tigrinum is an autumn flowering species, although many of its hybrids tend to bloom later. In recent years *Oncidium tigrinum* is being used more and more to produce these excellent brightly coloured intergeneric hybrids. This particular variety was raised by Mansell & Hatcher in Britain in 1973.

Paphiopedilum acmodontum

This is a mottled leaved species from the Philippines which should be grown under intermediate conditions, with a minimum night temperature of 55 °F (14 °C). It belongs to a large and varied group of *Paphiopedilum* species, all of which are easy to grow and flower freely during the winter months. They can be very successfully grown as house plants. They have a neat habit of growth and their mottled foliage is always attractive when the plant is not in bloom. They require a shady position and are intolerant of too much sunlight. Due to their lack of pseudo bulbs they should never be allowed to completely dry out, which will cause dehydration of the foliage. When their straightforward requirements are catered for, they are very rewarding plants to grow, and their colourful flowers will last for many weeks in perfection. Their distinctive pouch is the main feature of all the flowers which has given them the common name of 'Ladies Slipper Orchids'.

Paphiopedilum acmodontum produces a fairly tall stem with a single bloom. The plants are at their best when grown on to a large size which can be easily achieved within a few years.

While so many of the *Paphiopedilums* have been with us for many decades, this particular variety is a relatively recent introduction, and there still exists some controversy as to its exact location in the Philippines. However, although it has not been long in cultivation, it has quickly gained in popularity and is fortunately in plentiful supply at present. Already primary hybrids are being raised from *P. acmodontum* and it is proving to be a worthwhile parent.

Paphiopedilum fairieanum

This delightful species has a great history and caused a sensation by being discovered and then lost to cultivation for nearly fifty years. It was described in 1857, from a single plant owned by Mr. M. Fairie of Liverpool. But it was not until 1905 that it was reintroduced and became plentiful in cultivation. During those interval years when it was known but could not be found in the wild, there was much speculation and searching by the orchid collectors of that day. Finally, a reward of £1,000 (a great deal of money at that time) was offered by Sanders of St. Albans, England to anyone who could rediscover the *Paphiopedilum*.

Once in general cultivation this cool growing *Paphiopedilum* from the Himalayas became one of the great favourites of all time. No varietal forms were found until quite recently, and in 1975 a pure green variety was discovered. This beautiful variation was named *P. fairieanum* var. *concolor* 'Mont Millais' and was awarded an Award of Merit by the Royal Horticultural Society in September of that year. This green flowered variety is exceedingly rare, while the type remains a plentiful species.

Paphiopedilum fairieanum has been used tremendously in the raising of hybrids the earliest of these being very distinctive. With continuous breeding, much of its character was obscured in the later hybrids. Today there is some renewed interest in the primary hybrids from *P. fairieanum* and the old hybrids are appearing for the second time.

Paphiopedilum ciliolare, hennisianum and argus

This group includes three of the most popular of the mottled leaved *Paphiopedilum* species in cultivation today. They produce showy, long lasting blooms on slender stems. The flower on the left of the picture is *Paphiopedilum ciliolare*. This is a strong growing *Paphiopedilum* from Thailand and the Philippine islands from where it was introduced in 1882 by Stuart Low & Co., who were well known in those days as orchid importers. The species shows the powerful dark colouring which is so striking. In the early days of hybridising it was used considerably, although it is not a well known modern parent. The plant blooms during the spring months.

The flower to the right of the picture is *Paphiopedilum hennisianum*. This species comes from the Mindanao in the Philippines where it grows probably in the same habitat as *P. acmodontum*. These two species are almost identical in their foliage and difficult to tell apart when not in flower. Importations from the Philippines often contain plants of both species mixed together. *P. hennisianum* is an excellent grower and an ideal orchid for the beginner with sufficient warmth to meet its needs. It has not been greatly used in hybridisation, but can be most useful as a cut flower orchid.

The centre illustration is *Paphiopedilum argus*. This handsome species was introduced in 1872, and the name argus is derived from the eye like spots along the petals.

When first introduced these mottled leaved varieties were not considered to be the most important among the *Paphiopedilum* species, and they were not used for hybridising to the extent that the green leaved, Indian species were. Today, it is gratifying that the species is still abundant in the wild and good plants can be obtained to meet the demand for these handsome flowers.

Paphiopedilum appletonianum

This extremely dainty *Paphiopedilum* comes from Thailand and grows and blooms with great ease. The foliage is neat and handsomely mottled, and the flowers are carried singly, or occasionally two on a tall slender stem. It blooms during the early spring months and lasts for many weeks. It was used occasionally to produce primary hybrids, none of which are seen today, but in the last ten years it has been hybridised from more than in the last one hundred years. *P.* Adams Apple, *P.* Nisqually and *P.* Twinkle are a few of the primary hybrids which are once again creating a great deal of interest in Britain and the U.S.A.

Paphiopedilum appletonianum is an intermediate plant requiring a minimum night temperature of at least 55 °F (14 °C), with the equivalent daytime rise. It will grow in almost any shady situation, and can be seen at its best when left undivided and grown into a large plant.

Being handsome it makes a most attractive indoor plant when not in bloom. It will succeed well in a warm room provided it is kept well away from direct sources of heat and bright sunlight. Humidity trays are very useful for standing the plant on provided it is placed on an upturned saucer and not stood directly on the wet sand or gravel.

Paphiopedilum leucochilum

This captivating species represents a further group of *Paphiopedilums*, which belong to a sub genus known as *Brachypetalum*. Typical of species within this group is the well rounded flower, of basic white colouring, flowering from an extremely short stem, with the flower appearing to sit on the foliage. *P. leucochilum* produces a small, compact growing plant. The short leaved growths are extremely brittle and beautifully marbled with grey green. The species originates from Thailand where it can be found growing in crevices on the limestone cliffs within a few feet of the sea. Because of difficulty in collecting and the brittle leaves, imported plants are usually very poor specimens consisting of one or two broken leaves. It takes an experienced grower several years to produce a good plant from such a piece.

Paphiopedilum leucochilum is very closely related to another species, *P. godefroyae* and the two species are often considered to be the same, although the latter produces slightly smaller flowers. An imported batch will contain both plants together with varieties which appear half way between the two. This can make definite identification extremely difficult even when the plants are in bloom. These dwarf slipper orchids will readily interbreed with other *Paphiopedilums* and another closely related species, *P. bellatulum* was used considerably as a parent of many primary hybrids. Many of the modern coloured hybrids can trace their ancestry back to a species from this group, which has contributed a great deal to the eventual shape of the modern hybrid.

Paphiopedilum haynaldianum

This is a very handsome, large flowered species which belongs to a group of multi flowered *Paphiopedilums*, producing several blooms on one stem. It is a native of the Philippine Islands from where it was introduced in 1873. The plant is a large grower and produces long, strap like leaves. The flower spike is tall, and can carry from two to six flowers. As can be seen from the illustration these open one after another until the whole spray is fully open together, when they last for many weeks during the spring months. Although it is a green leaved *Paphiopedilum*, it is not a cool growing plant, and does best when grown in warm, moist conditions. It resents too much disturbance and is intolerant of continual division. It is at its best when allowed to grow into a specimen plant, although such plants can attain a considerable size, where space is limited.

Originally there was quite a lot of hybridising done with *P. haynaldianum*, but in more recent years interest in this plant as a parent appears to have declined. Therefore hybrids from it are rarely seen. However, one may imagine that while the species is lacking the favoured round shape, it should nevertheless have a considerable contribution to make by producing hybrids with more flowers on a stem. A spray of *Paphiopedilums* would surely win favour from the florists and growers.

Paphiopedilum philippinense

This is a further variety belonging to the group of multi flowered *Paphiopedilums*. It is a very handsome variety which comes from the Philippine islands, hence its name, and from where it was introduced in 1863. A little hybridising was done with this species in earlier days, as it was with all species. Our forefathers experimented by crossing as many different *Paphiopedilums* as possible. Some of the primary hybrids must have been very interesting and showy. None of these are in cultivation today, and it is very unlikely that these same crosses would ever be remade.

The flowers of *P. philippinense* open together on the stem, the elongated petals slowly uncurling from inside the opening bud. These petals are a most eyecatching feature of the flower, being held almost horizontally and twisting throught their length. It is a free flowering plant and again enjoys warm, humid conditions and is well worth growing into a specimen plant.

It has a very closely related species, *P. roebelinii*, with which it is sometimes considered to be synonymous, although most growers consider it a separate species which produces shorter petals and slightly smaller flowers.

Both the species *P. philippinense* and *P. haynaldianum* make similar growth and can be grown into large specimen plants if desired. Their long, strap-like leaves which are a dark, glossy green give them the appearance of a *Cymbidium*, and they will certainly take up as much room requiring a fairly large pot. Such specimen plants are capable of producing anything from ten to twelve stems, carrying perhaps a total of thirty flowers between them!

Paphiopedilum chamberlainianum var. primulinum

This elegant species, which in its short history has been known under several names, is now generally accepted as the above. It is a true concolor form of *P. chamberlainianum* and is a very modern discovery. It was unknown in the western world until 1972 when it was discovered in Sumatra. Several hundreds of plants were collected, these being sent to Britain, Europe and the U.S.A.. It can be considered as one of the latest and most important successful discoveries of a new species in the orchid world.

P. chamberlainianum var. *primulinum* belongs to a group of continuously flowering species, which produce their flowers in succession. As the illustration clearly shows, while one flower is open, the following bud is developing and will open a few days after the first flower has fallen. In this way many flowers are produced, extending the flowering season over many months, and over a year is not unusual. By this time the new growth has developed and is flowering in its turn. When the plant is large enough, it will remain continuously in flower.

The clear, yellow colouring could easily render this species a valuable parent plant of the future, and it will be interesting to see what hybrids are produced from it over the next few years.

The plant is a green leaved type, which requires hot house conditions where it is moist and shady.

When first introduced some plants were sold for as much as £50.00 sterling, but in the few short years since that time this orchid has become so plentiful it is well within the reach of any grower's pocket. The hybridist was quick to seize this new jewel for its potential breeding qualities. Already several nurseries are offering a number of seedlings incorporating this species.

Paphiopedilum Maudiae

This outstanding hybrid is probably the most widely grown *Paphiopedilum* in the world. It was registered by Charlesworth & Co., (of *Odontoglossum* fame) in 1900, when its parents were *P. callosum* var. *sanderae* and *P. lawrenceanum* var. *hyeanum*. Both these varieties were concolor forms of their type lacking the purple colouration. A coloured form was later produced using the same species. *P. callosum* and *P. lawrenceanum*. These were typical of their type and this cross is known as *P.* Maudiae 'Coloratum.' From *P.* Maudiae came several very fine distinct forms, and the best of these received awards from the Royal Horticultural Society. These varieties can still be found today, and the best is *P.* Maudiae 'Magnificium' FCC, also *P.* Maudiae 'The Queen' AM, both pure green.

Paphiopedilum Maudiae has also proved to be an excellent parent, and has produced a whole line of breeding of which the most well known is *P.* Claire de Lune. However, many of the hybrids from *P.* Maudiae have not become as consistently popular as *P.* Maudiae.

The flowers are amazingly long lasting and the plant is an extremely robust grower. It can be divided almost annually and will grow readily from single growths. It has probably been propagated from more than any other *Paphiopedilum*. Today it is grown by the thousand in Europe and the U.S.A. for the cut flower trade, all propagated without the advantages of meristemming. So free flowering is *P.* Maudiae that a single plant will regularly bloom twice a year, and where grown in a batch, one is seldom without blooms.

Paphiopedilums Maudiae 'Coloratum', Song of Mississippi and **glaucophyllum**

This interesting group of *Paphiopedilum* species and hybrids shows what can be achieved by primary hybridising. The left hand illustration is the hybrid, *P.* Maudiae 'Coloratum', the coloured form of the fore mentioned *P.* Maudiae. The right hand plant is a species, *P glaucophyllum.* This is one of the continuously flowering varieties, which produce a succession of blooms over a very long period. The plant is very closely related to *P. chamberlainianum* with which it is sometimes confused. The centre *Paphiopedilum* is Song of Mississippi and is a hybrid between *P.* Maudiae 'Coloratum' and *P. glaucophyllum.* Two separate clones are illustrated showing the influence from the two parents. The top variety with two flowers, is very similar to the species on the right, while the bottom clone is closer to the hybrid on the left. Both clones have inherited characteristics from each parent, and illustrate how much variation can be expected. Song of Mississippi is a very modern hybrid and was raised in 1975. It represents a novelty line of breeding in *Paphiopedilum* hybrids which is producing a refreshing combination of shape and colour.

These are all plants requiring intermediate conditions.

Paphiopedilum insigne, Harmachis and Colin Campbell

This is a group of *Paphiopedilums* which include the famous species, *P. insigne* at the bottom of the picture and two typical hybrids raised from it. Since its early introduction from India in 1820 *P. insigne* was to become one of the best known of all orchids. Its ease of culture and flowering ability made it immediately popular in all spheres. It was grown in its thousands for its cut flowers, which bloomed during the winter lasting for many weeks. It was equally prized by the 'window sill grower' possessing a single plant which, if left well alone would happily grow into a very large clump, which was then handed down from generation to generation.

There were at one time several varieties of *P. insigne*, including the most well known yellow variety, *P. insigne sanderae*. Of all the *Paphiopedilum* species, *P. insigne* was used the most for producing hybrids by their thousand, until today very few hybrids cannot trace back to this species. As with so many beautiful orchids which were extremely plentiful in years gone by, it is now becoming quite rare. It is impossible to import good strong specimens from the wild, and plants in cultivation are divisions or propagations of plants imported years ago.

The two hybrids with *P. insigne* are, *P.* Colin Campbell on the left and *P.* Harmachis on the right. Both these hybrids are over thirty years old and illustrate the typical breeding lines which were emerging from *P. insigne* and other species. Compare these two hybrids with the next picture but one which shows the improvement of the hybrids since that time. In addition to *P. insigne*, the other species which have helped to shape these hybrids are *P. spicerianum*, *P. villosum* as well as *P. godefroyae*.

These modern hybrids with their long stems are extremely popular on the continent of Europe where they are raised and sold in their tens of thousands for the pot plant trade. The speed by which they can be produced by the nurserymen makes them a fine house plant at the right price, taking into consideration the length of time the flowers will last and also the high demand for their cut flowers provided they can be produced with long stems.

Paphiopedilum Bruno 'Model' AM

This striking hybrid was raised by Messrs Veitch in England in 1896, at a time when the *Paphiopedilum* species were being hybridised from in their hundreds, as the growers were continually expanding the variety to be found among the species. Many of the early hybrids have been lost for ever, while *P.* Bruno 'Model' has successfully survived to the present day, and can still be found in a few collections. These are from the original cross and are therefore propagations of very old plants. The parents of the cross were *P.* Leeanum and *P. spicerianum*. *P.* Leeanum is a primary hybrid between *P. spicerianum* and *P. insigne*. The two species and one hybrid which combined to produce *P.* Bruno were at one time extremely plentiful and among the top varieties grown for the cut flower in Britain. The primary hybrid, *P.* Leeanum is seldom seen today, and survives in a few collections, where they have become collectors items. Until a few years ago, the two species, *P. spicerianum* and *P. insigne* were easily imported from their native India. *P. insigne* was introduced in 1820 and there were several named varieties, of which the most distinct was the pure yellow variety, *P. insigne* var. *sanderae*. *P. spicerianum* was considered extremely rare when it was first discovered in 1878, but later was to become one of the most popular among the species.

Paphiopedilum Bruno 'Model' shows great influence from *P. spicerianum* as would be expected. It is a very robust grower, and blooms very freely during the winter. As well as being a most successful hybrid, *P.* Bruno has made its mark as an excellent parent.

Paphiopedilum F. C. Puddle FCC

This is a world famous hybrid among the white flowered varieties. It was produced in 1932 and was named after the famous orchid grower who was so closely associated with its breeding. Its parents were *P.* Actaeus and *P.* Astarte. The former was a hybrid from *P. insigne* and *P.* Leeanum which was registered in 1895 and a very old, primary hybrid. The yellow flowered variety of *P. insigne* var. *sanderae* would have probably been used in this instance. *P.* Astarte originated from two white species, *P. bellatulum* and the longer stemmed *P. niveum*. In *Paphiopedilum* F. C. Puddle we have the perfect combination of a beautifully shaped, almost pure white flower carried on a proportionally long stem. It clearly shows much influence from *P. niveum* in its colour and size of flower, while the *P. spicerianum* has disappeared altogether.

    P. F. C. Puddle was considered a most outstanding *Paphiopedilum* hybrid in its day, and was awarded the First Class Certificate by the Royal Horticultural Society. Today it is still a greatly sought after hybrid which has lost nothing with the passing of years. It is a neat, compact grower with slightly mottled foliage which enjoys the warm, moist conditions consistent with its Thai origins. It has progressed through the years to become a most important parent in the production of further white hybrids.

Paphiopedilum Geelong

This handsome hybrid illustrates the typical and most plentiful type of *Paphiopedilum* grown today. It has been produced through many generations of hybrids tracing back to a modestly few species which include, not surprisingly, *P. insigne* and *P. spicerianum* which, among others, have contributed the rich colouring and spotted dorsal petal. The fairly short stem and solid round flower has come, again through many generations, from the species *P. bellatulum*, which is a stemless, white flowered species belonging to the sub genus *Brachypetalum*, of which *P. leucochilum* as previously described, is another typical example. *P. bellatulum* is a dwarf growing species, slow growing and requiring hot house culture. Traces of its beautifully marbled foliage can frequently be seen in the foliage of the modern hybrid such as *P.* Geelong, and for this reason they grow at their best in fairly hot and shady conditions.

Paphiopedilum Geelong was raised in 1966 by R. & E. Ratcliffe Ltd., in Britain from the parents *P.* Rollright and *P.* Canberra. It has in turn been used considerably for breeding equally fine hybrids of its type. These differ from other popular genera in that the seed pods contain very few seeds compared with the average orchid pod. For this reason hybridisers may produce up to a thousand pods in one season, and of the resulting seedlings, there will be only a few of each cross.

To date *Paphiopedilums* have failed to mass produce by meristemming. The fastest method of producing new stock remains conventional seed raising. As the world's demand for these fascinating orchids increases, so the nurserymen produce more plants, with the result that tremendous strides are being made in the shape, size and colour of the blooms, as well as the length of their stems.

Phragmipedium Sedenii

The *Phragmipediums* are a separate genus closely related to the *Paphiopedilums*, and at one time incorrectly combined with them under the genus *Cypripedium*. Among the *Phragmipediums* can be found some extremely beautiful and curious orchids, many of them very rare today. They will not usually interbreed with the *Paphiopedilums* although a few bigeneric crosses between them have been recorded in the past. Today, very little hybridising is done with *Phragmipediums* and the few hybrids which are occasiaonlly seen in cultivation are propagations of very old plants raised at the turn of the century. No doubt some of these early hybrids were very handsome plants, and it is a sad fact that there are many fewer *Phragmipediums* in cultivation today.

Phragmipedium Sedenii is one of the very early hybrids, raised in 1873 by the well known orchid importers and raisers of that time, Messrs Veitch & Co.. Its parents were *P. schlimii* and *P. longifolium*, two species originating from Central America. Both the parents and the hybrid are extremely rare today.

P. Sedenii remains continuously in flower producing more flowers from a single stem. The illustration shows a large specimen plant flowering at its best with several large, flowering stems. It is a most beautiful and distinct variety which enjoys intermediate house conditions. From being once very plentiful, it has now become a rare collectors item.

For the second time in one hundred years *Phragmipediums* are coming to the fore as once again great interest is being shown in them. The result is that hybrids from them are starting to be made all over again, and rare species which were at one time plentiful, are being raised from seed. All this after many years of neglect of the genus. There appears to be a slight possibility that with this genus there may be more success with meristemming in which case we could see a rapid and welcome return of some of the older varieties which will be found in earlier orchid books under the name *Selenipedium*.

Paphiopedilum Delrosi

This unique *Paphiopedilum* is a first generation hybrid between two extraordinary species, *P. rothschildianum* and *P. delenatii*. It was raised in France by Vacherot & Lecoufle and registered by them in 1961. The *P. rothschildianum* was introduced from New Guinea in 1888, when it was described as a 'most astonishing introduction' of that era. From that time it was used tremendously as a parent and very soon hybrids from it were plentiful, although these have since disappeared. The striking flowers of *P. rothschildianum* are large, highly coloured and boldly striped. The lateral petals are long and narrow, extending almost horizontally as in the related species, *P. philippinense*. It has always been a rare plant in cultivation.

The other parent is *P. delenatii*, a beautiful, pink flowered type, totally different from *P. rothschildianum*. *P. delenatii* is a native of Vietnam and is therefore impossible to obtain today. However, it has proved to be easy to raise from seed and nursery plants are plentiful.

The flower of *P.* Delrosi shows clearly the influence from both of its distinguished parents. From *P. rothschildianum* has come the overall striping of the flower, while the beautiful soft pink colouring is inherited from *P. delenatii*. The latter is a small growing plant with well mottled foliage in contrast to the large, green foliage of *P. rothschildianum*. *P.* Delrosi has inherited a type of growth midway between. It enjoys hot conditions, but grows slowly.

The plant represents a fairly new trend in pink flowered *Paphiopedilums* of which several fine hybrids have been produced from *P. delenatii*.

Phalaenopsis intermedia

This natural hybrid carries its flowers on long arching sprays and the flowers open a few at a time while the spike continues to grow. It can be seen from the illustration that a few flowers are open on the spray which have many more buds developing in succession. In this way it will remain in bloom for several months through the winter and spring. The plant is considered to be a natural hybrid between *P. amabilis* and *P. equestris*. The latter being a small flowered species with rosy pink flowers.

The first introduction of *P. intermedia* was from a single plant found among an importation of *P. aphrodite* (syn. *P. amabilis*) in 1852. Later, in 1861 two more appeared in a further importation. It remained an extremely rare plant until the cross using *P. amabilis* and *P. equestris* was made in 1886 and the resulting plants of *P. intermedia* confirmed this natural hybrid.

The most outstanding feature of *P. intermedia* is the rosy pink, self coloured lip from which has come the modern red lipped *Phalaenopsis* which makes a welcome variation to the ordinary white flowers.

Phalaenopsis leuchorroda

This is a supposed natural hybrid from two separate species, *P. aphrodite* and *P. schillerana*. The plants obtained today appear to differ considerably from the older forms previously grown. Our modern version carries very distinct yellow side lobes to the lip, which in earlier described types is said to be mainly rose purple. Before the turn of the century, two varieties of the type were recorded, neither of which resembles the present day species.

It was first imported from the Philippines by Stuart Low & Co., in 1874, among an importation of its supposed parents.

P. leuchorroda produces a neat plant with mottled grey foliage. It was used for hybridising with the other main *Phalaenopsis* species with which it quickly became merged along with other, almost identical hybrids. Today it is grown mainly by collectors of *Phalaenopsis* species but it is still a striking flower with the unusual yellow side lobes to the lip. It blooms freely during the autumn and winter months.

When the flowers are finished and have become papery prior to dropping off, the stem will remain bare, but in a green state. Careful examination of the stem will show there are several dormant buds, probably four or five between the base of the plant and the first flowers. If the stem is cut back to one of these eyes, a new spike will develop and within a few weeks the plant will once again be in flower. Provided the plant is strong enough it can be allowed to remain in bloom for several months without harming the plant.

Phalaenopsis amabilis

This illustration shows two excellent examples of the species, *P. amabilis*. It is a highly variable plant which blooms during the winter months. There were at one time several names attributed to this species which resulted in considerable confusion in the subsequent registration of new hybrids. This was righted in 1969 when all the *Phalaenopsis* species were completely revised and brought up to date. *Phalaenopsis aphrodite, P. formosa* and *P. rimestadiana*, which were originally described as separate species, were all considered varietal forms of *P. amabilis*.

Of these varieties, *P. amabilis* was mostly favoured by the early hybridists who crossed it with just about every other *Phalaenopsis* species known at that time. The large, modern white hybrids which have become so plentiful can all be traced back to this white species. Some of the earliest hybrids where the above names had been used were not hybrids at all, but merely line breeding from variations of a single species.

This being a winter blooming orchid, there is always the danger of bud drop at this time of the year. One should bear in mind that the buds are the most sensitive part of the plant and and excessive imbalance of the conditions will cause bud loss. This is usually a cultural fault rather than anything else. Too high or too low a temperature is the main cause of this complaint, as also over- or underwatering, all of which contribute to bud drop. Therefore a careful check upon the conditions will determine where the grower is going wrong.

Phalaenopsis stuartiana

This extremely handsome species, has always been one of the most favoured among the *Phalaenopsis*. The plant has striking mottled foliage and long, strap like leaves. It blooms very freely during the winter months, producing one, or on a large plant easily two, branching flower spikes. These are many flowered, the individual blooms fairly small, and beautifully spotted on their lips and lower petals.

The plant was first introduced from Mindanao in 1881 by the famous old firm of Stuart Low & Co., in England, after whom it was named. As a parent it was used considerably to produce many of the early hybrids which carried the distinctive spotting through successive generations to become the famous 'leopard lips' of modern French breeding.

Unlike other *Phalaenopsis* species which became confused with each other, and later were considered to be one and the same, *P. stuartiana* is more distinct. It has one closely related species in *P. schillerana* which also carries similar, but finer, spotting on the lower petals and lip. The main difference between the two species is their colouring. *P. schillerana* is rosy pink while the smaller flowers of *P. stuartiana* are pure white except for the spotting.

Many breeders are returning to *P. stuartiana* in order to increase the number of blooms on a spike. They also value its frequent habit of branching which can be carried forward into its hybrids. The illustration shows a single spray although more often than not the species will branch. Hopefully, from this species will come in the near future a new and exciting line of breeding producing the multi flowered *Phalaenopsis* with masses of medium sized flowers on compact and branching spikes. These plants will be bred especially for the pot plant trade and will be perpetually blooming.

Phalaenopsis equestris and cornu cervi

Phalaenopsis equestris to the left of the picture is seen here in its two distinct coloured forms. The plant is a typical miniature *Phalaenopsis* and can be grown in a hot greenhouse, or makes an ideal subject for an indoor growing case. It was first described in 1848 having been imported from the Philippine islands. It was at one time known as *P. rosea*. Today, the forementioned name is generally accepted. This species has been responsible for much breeding with the larger species, where natural hybrids from it are known to occur, and with later hybrids to produce some of the novelty and different crosses seen recently.

Phalaenopsis cornu cervi on the right hand side of the photograph is a further example of a miniature *Phalaenopsis*. This particular species readily propagates itself by producing young plants along the old flower stems. Although the individual blooms are small and not over showy, it blooms very freely and is a most rewarding plant to grow, taking up little room in the greenhouse or indoor growing case. It was first described in 1887 coming from Moulmein. Being a less conspicuous *Phalaenopsis* it has not been used for hybridising to the same extent as others of the genus. A mature plant will remain in bloom for long periods, with just a few flowers open at a time.

Phalaenopsis Lipperose

This fine hybrid with pink origins represents a breakthrough in the breeding of these *Phalaenopsis*, which previously lacked in size and shape of flower and could not compare with the superior quality of the white flowered types. For many years the quality of *Phalaenopsis* hybrids had been led by the whites. During the past few years some excellent German breeding has succeeded in increasing the size of the pinks, until they can now compare with the whites, and huge round flowers are appearing with many flowers on a spike.

Phalaenopsis Lipperose is a typical hybrid which has emerged from a long line of selective pink breeding, much of it being done by Fritz Hark in Germany. Its parents are Ruby Wells and Zada, the latter a very important hybrid. The cross was registered in 1968, since when it has been so successful it has been remade several times by various growers, and from these have come some awarded plants.

The illustration shows a seedling flowering for the first time on a young plant, and therefore not carrying many flowers. It is a flower which shows much promise and on a large, mature plant could well be of award standard.

Phalaenopsis sanderana

This *Phalaenopsis* is among the most beautiful of the species within its group. It is sometimes considered to be a natural hybrid between *P. schillerana* and *P. amabilis*, although for horticultural purposes it remains listed as a separate species. Its flowers are certainly to be considered as halfway betwen the two. It was first introduced from its native Philippines during 1882, when it was reported growing upon the trunks and branches of trees close to the sea shore. The discoverer was a famous name of those days, Roebelin, a well known collector whose name was perpetuated in the species, *Paphiopedilum roebelinii*. The plants were sent to the famous old firm of Sanders, and named in honour of the founder of that great firm.

It is not noted to be a variable species, although following its introduction a pure white form was described which was given the varietal name *alba*. This plant was probably a once only occurence which has not been seen in cultivation since then.

The flowers of *P. sanderana* are a beautiful soft pink and its long, branching spikes ensure that it will remain forever in the eye of the enthusiast. The plant is also attractive with its large, broad leaves which may be dark green or lightly mottled with grey, especially when the leaf is young

Apart from its desirability as a species, *P. sanderana* has contributed greatly towards the pink coloured hybrids of today. The early pink hybrids were smaller and not so well shaped as the whites, and therefore lacked in popularity until this could be improved by further breeding.

Phalaenopsis Hokuspokus

This excellent hybrid has been produced with the combination of two separate lines of breeding. Its parents are *P*. Lipperosa, as just described, and *P*. Francine, which is the result of a famous French line of breeding producing their famous 'leopard lips'. These colourful types have come through many generations from the dominant species, *P. stuartiana. P.* Hokuspokus is a german bred hybrid, registered in 1974. The different colours of the parents have produced a varied hybrid from which have come a range of shades, from pure white, through the pastel pinks, always with the heavy patterning and spotting of the lip and lower sepals. From its ancestor, *P. stuartiana* also comes the freely branching habit, while the pink colouring sometimes evident is from *P. schillerana.*

P. Hokuspokus has already proved to be a most exciting hybrid, but it has yet to prove itself a good parent, and it will be a plant well worth looking out for among the parents of the next generations of leopard lip *Phalaenopsis.*

This illustration shows a cane supporting the flower spikes. This is essential for all *Phalaenopsis* with large spikes. The blooms can be extremely heavy and need some support to keep them upright to the base of the buds. A thin bamboo cane should be inserted into the compost and to this the young developing spike can be tied. From the base of the buds the spike can usually be left to form its natural arch when the flowers will all show the same face with overlapping petals.

Phalaenopsis Latone

This is an older hybrid made in France in 1953 from two white hybrids, *P.* Blizzard and *P.* San Marino. Its size and shape was exceptional for that time, and firmly established the modern quality which has come to be expected of the whites. The many generations of line breeding from selected varieties of *P. amabilis* have led to the formation and width of the petals which almost meet at the top of the flower. The lip also is white, with the faintest touch of yellow at the base. This has made it an excellent bloom for the cut flower trade and is in great demand by florists all over Europe who dye the flowers different colours according to the demand.

Phalaenopsis hybrids can be induced to flower at almost any time of the year. By dropping their night time temperature by a few degrees for about a week it is possible to encourage the embryo flower spikes into activity. However, it would be dangerous and not necessary to reduce the temperature inside the *Phalaenopsis* house where there may be young seedlings which could be harmed by the reduction in their heating requirements. Rather, selected mature plants should be removed to the colder *Cymbidium* section, to be returned after one week. If the temperature check has had the desired effect, the flower spikes will appear after ten days. It is not advisable to leave the plants in the lower temperature for too long, as this will produce spotting or other damage to the foliage. To prevent this the plant should not be watered for the period it is to be rested. Generally, temperatures which are lower than those recommended for *Phalaenopsis* can be dangerous to the plants over a prolonged period, and should not be risked.

Phalaenopsis Halle

This is a first generation, primary hybrid produced by crossing the species, *P. equestris* with a white hybrid, *P.* Keith Shaffer. It was raised in Germany in 1972. *P. equestris* is a minaiture *Phalaenopsis* which carries its small, pink blooms on well flowered arching sprays. It is a variable species, and the colour can differ from a light to rosy pink, while the lip can be deep pink or brick red. It is very popular as a species and has also helped to produce some very pretty novelty hybrids. In the hybrid *P.* Halle, the more dominant parent has been the hybrid, *P.* Keith Shaffer which is a famous American product noted for its large, rounded flower, of good texture. The advantages of taking such an excellent modern hybrid back to a species is clearly evident in *P.* Halle. The flowers are much smaller than the foregoing *P.* Latone and its size is between the large hybrid and the miniature species. The flowers contain the faintest flush of pink, which has spread over the lip. This beautiful combination on an elegantly arching spike, is getting very slightly away from the conventional.

The flowers on the hybrids are extremely long lasting, and can remain in perfection for up to three months. The danger, particularly with the white varieties, is that they can easily show damp marks after a few weeks. During the winter months and periods of high humidity and poor light, such spotting of the flowers can occur. For this there is no cure, and prevention is the answer. No *Phalaenopsis* house is complete without a circulating fan to keep the air moving. This will not harm the blooms, even if they are in the direct path of the air flow causing them to wave about.

Phalaenopsis Artur Elle

This delightful little hybrid represents a quite different type of *Phalaenopsis* which is rapidly gaining in popularity today. It is totally unlike the previously mentioned types and is the result of crossing one conventional type of *Phalaenopsis*, *P*. Mad Hatter, with a species of the *P. lueddemanniana* group. This is *P. mariae*, a small but highly coloured species which produces a limited number of flowers on a spike. These are star shaped and they last well. It has always been a popular species for growing where space is limited, and is now proving a most noteworthy hybrid with this type of novelty crossing. On the other side of *P*. Artur Elle is a large, white conventional hybrid from *P*. Mad Hatter which has proved an important parent when crossed with many different *Phalaenopsis*. The cross was made in Germany by Herr Wichmann in 1971. The illustration shows two different seedlings, with clearly marked differences between them. The hybrid is an excellent plant for a small enclosed environment such as an indoor growing case where headroom is limited.

Phalaenopsis Barbara Moler

This is one further illustration of the results achieved by crossing the conventional type of *Phalaenopsis* back to a miniature species. In this variety the two distinct species of *P. fasciata* and *P. lueddemanniana* are represented, with *P. lueddemanniana* being the most dominant in the shape of the flower and spike, and also the overall delicate spotting. These novelty hybrids have a great future and we shall no doubt be seeing many more of them in the next few years. This is an American hybrid raised in 1971 by Charles Beard in Florida.

    P. Barbara Moler will continue flowering for months at a time, repeating the flowering habit of *P. lueddemanniana*, by producing a succession of blooms from a continuously growing spike.

Phalaenopsis Golden Sands 'Miami Shores'

Among the *Phalaenopsis* the yellow colouring is only found within a few species from the *P. lueddemanniana* group. This has made the breeding of yellow *Phalaenopsis* almost impossible and little success has been achieved until a few years ago. The yellow *Phalaenopsis* come from *P. lueddemanniana*, and are therefore lacking in shape. *P.* Golden Sands is considered to be the finest of all the yellow flowered *Phalaenopsis* hybrids. Its shape has come through very strongly from the conventional white breeding behind it on one side, combining with *P. lueddemanniana* in this winning combination. The white parent is an American hybrid, *P.* Fenton Davis Advant.

P. Golden Sands has been successfully meristemmed, and therefore good propagations are readily available, although these are expensive as one would expect for the best of its type in the world. It has also been used as a parent to produce such American hybrids as *P.* Apple Sauce and *P.* Cream Puff, although these varieties have not been seen by the authors, it would appear from their names, that some of the fine yellowing has become lost in one further generation.

The illustration shows a young meristemmed plant flowering for the first time. Although more flowers will be produced on a larger plant, these will come in succession over a long period of time, with never very many open at a time. Its fine colouring is consistent with good culture, and if not well grown the yellow becomes less noticeable. This plant was raised in the U.S.A. in 1964 where it has been awarded. In Britain it has also become very highly acclaimed.

Doritaenopsis Malibu

Some very interesting breeding has been done with *Phalaenopsis* and their allied genera. *Doritaenopsis* is a bigeneric cross between *Phalaenopsis* and *Doritis*. The genus *Doritis* was created for a single species, *D. pulcherrima*, which was at one time included with the *Phalaenopsis*. The species is highly variable and the most colourful of these are deep mauve. When this species is crossed with pink *Phalaenopsis*, the result can be very colourful, as can be seen with *D*. Malibu. This excellent hybrid was raised in the U.S.A. in 1962 and shows the greater influence from *D. pulcherrima*. The upright spikes are many flowered, small and highly coloured as in the species. The buds at the top of the spike will not open for several weeks, by which time the lower flowers will have finished and dropped off, thus it will continue to flower for several months at a time.

The *Phalaenopsis* parent of *D*. Malibu is *P*. Algeriana, a hybrid which is only two generations away from four species which are, *P. aphrodite, P. sanderana, P. equestris* and *P. schillerana*. The bigeneric *D*. Malibu has inherited much of the vigour from these species and is also very free flowering.

Experiments in breeding have produced a number of variations in the colour of the *Doritaenopsis*, although the rich pinks and mauve remain the most popular. The cultural requirements of *Doritaenopsis* are the same as for the *Phalaenopsis* and they can be grown side by side. The *Doritaenopsis* differ slightly in their appearance from the *Phalaenopsis* by producing a greater number of leaves at a time which are more upright in habit and are narrower and pointed. Their flowering ability is astounding! On a small plant two flower spikes at a time are not uncommon. Larger plants may carry several tall, branching spikes at one prolonged flowering.

Doritaenopsis Shirley Janes

In this modern British raised *Doritaenopsis* the *Phalaenopsis* side of the cross has been more dominant than *Doritis pulcherrima*. The *Phalaenopsis* parent used was *P.* Sourire, a very fine pink hybrid of French origin which has influenced the spotting of the petals. The result is a larger flower resembling *Phalaenopsis*, and the long, arching spray of flowers, which will remain in bloom for many weeks. The *Doritis* is very evident in the shape and colouring of the lip.

   The cross was made by Peter Janes, a leading amateur grower and breeder from Solihull in 1974.

Sophronitis coccinea

Although a small species of modest size, this is a most outstanding little plant which should be represented wherever orchids are grown. One of its most commanding features is the vivid red colouring which has made the species one of the most important members of its sub tribe. It will readily interbreed with other related plants, when the rich colouring is carried forward with breathtaking results. Some of the man made genera which include *S. coccinea* as one parent are *Sophrocattleya*, *Sophrolaelia* and *Epiphronitis*. There are many other multigeneric hybrids which incorporate several genera. One example is the genus *Potinara*, the first of which was made in 1922, using *Brassavola* (*Rhyncholaelia*), *Cattleya, Laelia* and *Sophronitis*.

Sophronitis coccinea is the showiest member of an extremely small genus, represented by a mere half dozen species. It was introduced into Britain in 1837 from its native Brazil, where it was discovered growing at high altitudes where early morning frosts were known to occur. The plant was introduced as *S. grandiflora*, a name by which it is still known horticulturally. However, its correct botanical name is *S. coccinea* which was formerly considered to be a separate species. For the registration of hybrids *S. coccinea* has been used since 1961.

Normal, cool house culture is suitable for *S. coccinea*, with particular care taken with the watering of the plant. Being of small stature it cannot cope with extreme dryness or overwatering to any extent. It should be kept evenly moist while growing and on the dry side while showing no growth during the resting season.

Rhyncholaelia digbyana

This species represents another notable member of the sub tribe *Laeliinae*. While being a most beautiful and distinct orchid, its greatest value has been in its contribution to the breeding of multi generic hybrids within the sub tribe. From this single species has come the large, frilly lips to be found on the majority of modern *Cattleya* hybrids.

The species was introduced from Honduras in 1846, although it also inhabits dry regions of Mexico and Guatemala. It was classified as *Brassavola digbyana* and later removed to the genus *Laelia*. Today, while it is still horticulturally known as *Brassavola*, it is botanically more correctly *Rhyncholaelia digbyana*. This genus was especially created for this species and one other, *R. glauca*. The flowers of the latter are similarly beautiful in their delicate colouring, but the lip is rounded and lacks the deep fringe. For registration purposes the new name of *R. digbyana* has been used since 1971.

Rhyncholaelia digbyana does best when grown in the intermediate section of the greenhouse, or a warm sunny room. It requires the minimum of shade, the tough, grey green foliage being adapted to withstand the direct sun to some extent. The plant can be shy flowering if insufficient sunlight is given. The plant should never be overwatered, and prefers to be on the dry side while growing, with a completely dry rest when inactive. Otherwise, its general culture remains the same as for other members of the sub tribe.

The extraordinary and very beautiful deep fringe on the lip is unique to this genus and found on no other plant within the sub tribe. It is also a highly unusual feature to be found anywhere in orchids. In the numerous hybrids obtained from the species this fringe is modified into a lacey or frilly lip, the deep fringe always being partially lost. One other important contribution of the *Rhyncholaelias* to intergeneric hybrids is the greatly sought after green colouring. The green *Brassocattleyas* have a great future, and we feel sure more of them will be making their appearance in the years to come.

Cattleya Bob Betts

Among the species of the *Cattleyas* and *Laelias* albino forms are fairly common, and these natural variants were used widely to produce the different coloured hybrids. *Cattleya* Bob Betts is a typical white hybrid of good quality which has come from selected line breeding using these albino varieties. The species involved with the original crossing were *Cattleya gaskelliana* var. *alba* and *Cattleya mossiae* 'Hye'. This cross was named *C.* Suzanne Hye, and since 1906 when it was registered, figured predominantly in the pedigree of *C.* Bob Betts. Its parent was a very famous white in its time. *C.* Bow Bells, which was used extensively for hybridising further excellent whites. The other parent of *C.* Bob Betts was, surprisingly, the white form of *C. mossiae*. This back crossing to the species has improved the vigour of the plant as well as the substance of the flower. *Cattleya* Bob Betts is an american hybrid, raised by McDade in 1950. It shows the tremendous strides which have been taken with the four generations of breeding which it has taken from the species.

Cattleya Cotelle

This showy hybrid has been achieved by pure breeding from *Cattleya* species, with no influence from other related genera. Its breeding lines are very similar to the previously mentioned *Cattleya* Bob Betts, but using the coloured types rather than the selected albino forms. This has retained the wonderful richness of colouring and improved the shape and texture of the flowers. This hybrid was registered by David Sanders Orchids Ltd., in 1968. Its parents were *Cattleya* Cowaniae and *Cattleya* Estelle. Both these hybrids can be traced back to the species, *Cattleya mossiae* and *Cattleya warneri*, which were crossed to produce *Cattleya* Intertexta, an old primary hybrid made in 1897 by Veitch.

    Cattleya Cotelle is beautifully fragrant and blooms during the months of December and January. It is an excellent hybrid for the amateur who enjoys entering his or her orchids for competition.

Cattleya Capra

This handsome hybrid is a first generation cross between the two species *Cattleya amethystoglossa* and *Cattleya labiata*. It was originally raised as long ago as 1910 by the famous British firm of Charlesworth & Co. This fine old *Cattleya* has been remade in recent years, using two fine blue forms; *C. labiata* var. *coerulea* and *C. amethystoglossa* 'blue'.

The parents, which were so plentiful when this cross was first made, are today, along with most other *Cattleya* species, rare in cultivation and grown lovingly by a few enthusiasts who go to great lengths to procure them mainly for breeding purposes.

The dominant species in this cross is *C. labiata* var. *coerulea*. This type was at one time highly variable and consisted of several named varieties. It was introduced in 1818 from Brazil and was used repeatedly in the breeding of early hybrids. The plant belongs to the unifoliate type of *Cattleya*, having a single leaf to each bulb. It produces its beautiful, fragrant blooms during the late autumn months. The other parent of *C.* Capra is a species of the bifoliate group. These produce slender pseudo bulbs which can attain considerable length more reminiscent of canes. These are topped by a pair of stout leaves, from the centre of which come the flowers, produced on large heads, being smaller and heavier textured than those from the unifoliate group. *C. amethystoglossa* usually has rose lilac coloured flowers, the petals and sepals spotted with purple. The plant takes its name from the vivid amethyst colouring of the lip, which can vary according to the variety.

Laeliocattleya Lykas

This colourful hybrid can trace its origins back to 1885, when its first hybrid ancestor was registered. This was the primary hybrid *Laeliocattleya* Canhamiane, from the two species *Cattleya mossiae* and *Laelia purpurata*. Six generations of further breeding incorporating *Cattleya trianae* and *Cattleya dowiana* among other species and several further hybrids, produced *L.* Lykas which was registered in France in 1956 by Vacherot & Lecoufle. The hybrid is typical of this bigeneric genus which has become tremendously popular the world over. It is widely grown in its thousands for the cut flower trade, as well as the plant trade. Its strong fragrance adding greatly to its appeal.

L. Lykas is a strong, robust grower which blooms freely during the late autumn months.

This hybrid, and the many others almost identical to it, are freely available, often as seedlings of various ages, or as meristemmed plants which guarantee the quality of the plant obtained. The plant illustrated has two flowers, but a larger plant can produce twice this number.

Brassocattleya Thalie

This bigeneric hybrid shows clearly the difference obtained by crossing a *Cattleya* with the *Brassavola* (*Rhyncholaelia*) *digbyana*. Two *Cattleya* species which can be found in the makeup of *B*. Thalie are *C. mossiae* and *C. gaskelliana*, the rich mauve coloured varieties. Further along the family tree the parents of *B*. Thalie are *B*. Deesse and *C*. Opalisque. This cross, from a famous line of french breeding, was made in 1955. The parent *B*. Deesse is a very well known hybrid from which have come several awarded varieties. The flowers are snow white of exceptional shape and texture.

B. Thalie has inherited this excellent shape and substance from its famous parent which has toned the rich purples to the beautiful soft pink which makes *B*. Thalie such an eyecatching hybrid. The round, opened lip is typical of the hybrids produced from the species *R. digbyana*.

Fifty years ago these and similar large flowered hybrids were in great demand for corsages and bridal bouquets. However, with the modern day trend for smaller arrangements these beautiful orchids are considered too large for the majority of florist's work. Nevertheless, they will always remain among the most popular orchids for the amateur grower and the show bench. These beautiful but heavy blooms cannot be seen to their full advantage without the added support of a split cane at the back of the flower.

Potinara Cherub 'Spring Daffodil'

This charming and beautiful multigeneric hybrid contains four separate genera. The main species involved with the making of Cherub are *Sophronitis coccinea*, whose influence can be seen partly in the shape of the lip, although the red colouring so predominant among the *Potinaras* has been replaced by the rich yellow, *Laelia cinnabarina*, a small but highly coloured Laelia which produces a number of starry flowers from a slender stem, *Rhyncholaelia (Brassavola) digbyana*, of which little can be seen in the flower, and *Cattleya aurantiaca*. This latter is a small flowered, but brightly coloured species, which produces a cluster of orange flowers. *Cattleya aurantiaca* has perhaps been the most dominant species.

Potinara Cherub 'Spring Daffodil' was raised in the U.S.A. by Stewards in 1965. The plant is unique not only for its superb colouring, but also for the way in which it came about. *P.* Cherub has been achieved with the minimum of hybridising, and it is worth taking a look at its remarkably short but successful family tree:

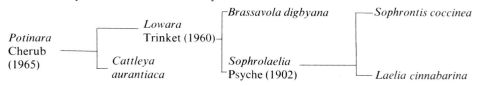

Sophrolaeliocattleya Phena 'Saturn'

This is a trigeneric hybrid incorporating the genera of *Sophronitis, Laelia* and *Cattleya*. The colouration from *S. coccinea* has been retained through four generations of breeding, while the size of the flower is consistant with the influence from the *Laelia* and *Cattleya*. One further species used as a grandparent of *S.* Phena is *C. dowiana*. This beautiful species, extremely rare today, was used repeatedly in the hybridising of early hybrids, and become the most important parent in the production of yellow hybrids. The flowers of *C. dowiana* are a rich yellow, with a highly coloured lip richly decorated in mauve purple. This flamboyantly coloured lip has been continued and intensified in all its progeny and can be seen in many modern hybrids.

S. Phena was raised in 1930 and its variety 'Saturn' was in great demand at a time when conventional propagation produced a very limited number of plants over a period of several years. Today, it is still considered to be one of the more superior among the red Cattleyas, and is now readily available as a meristemmed plant.

Dendrobium nobile

The *Dendrobiums* are an extremely large and varied genus of orchids which are widely distributed throughout the Old World. They have always ranked among the most popular genera, many of the species being exceptionally beautiful and amidst a host of latter day hybrids remain the most widely grown. Their type of growth is dissimilar from other orchids in their pseudo bulbs which have become elongated into canes to a greater or lesser extent.

Dendrobium nobile is a variable species, which blooms the length of the previous year's bulbs during the spring. It was introduced to Britain from India and first flowered in 1837. Since that time it has been used extensively for hybridising among similar related species, and later crossing with the early hybrids. This resulted in a host of hybrids all of which were very similar to each other. In recent years more notable hybridisng has been achieved, particularly in Japan, where the size and shape of the flowers has been much improved, while the colour range has been extended to include rich lavenders, reds, whites and yellows. These hybrids are not always as free flowering as the species, and require plenty of light particularly during the shorter months of the year to achieve peak flowering.

Dendrobium nobile has always been an easily obtained species, and is far more widely grown than its higher classed hybrids. It is an easy and inexpensive orchid for the beginner, and can also be used for its flowers which will last well in water.

The winter culture of *Dendrobium nobile* is particularly important if the plant is to bloom well the following spring. It should be given a good dry rest with maximum light to ripen the long, bamboo like canes. When the flower buds are seen emerging from the nodes along the bulb the plant should remain dry until these can be distinguished as buds. Water applied too soon at this stage can turn these embryo buds into adventitious growths, which is an ideal method of propagating, but at the expense of flowers. By the time the buds are developing well, the new growth should be seen at the base, and watering can recommence for the growing season. During the summer the plants thrive in a warm, humid atmosphere with plenty of water to the roots. These conditions will encourage a good, fast growth which should be completed with the approach of winter. Generally, *Dendrobium nobile* is a cool house orchid and will succeed well in a minimum winter night temperature of 50 °F (10 °C) with higher summer temperatures while the plant is growing.

Dendrobium nobile var. virginale

There were at one time a number of distinct varietal forms of *Dendrobium nobile*. Of these, the most outstanding is the pure white form, *D. nobile* var. *virginale*. It is not unusual among *Dendrobiums* of the *nobile* type to find the albino forms, albeit that they remain rare. The flowers lack any trace of the rich purple colouring of the type, only the lip is creamy white. The plant grows and flowers as easily as the type, and when first discovered was an extremely rare plant. Today, nursery raised plants ensure that the plant continues to flourish and it is not now as rare as it was in the past.

From *D. nobile* var. *virginale* have come some excellent white hybrids, many with coloured lips and differing features.

Dendrobium williamsoni

This is another pretty species belonging to the same group and therefore related to *Dendrobium infundibulum*. It was probably introduced into Britain about the same time, but was not considered a very important species at that time. The plant produces short, stout pseudo bulbs and requires the same cool house treatment as *D. infundibulum*. It blooms during the spring and early summer months, when the flowers appear from the top of the bulbs. These are produced in profusion, are smaller than *D. infundibulum*, but extremely showy with their gaily coloured lips. They are also fragrant, and long lasting. The plant will grow quite happily in a pot, or may be cultivated on a piece of cork bark which makes the plant into a very attractive specimen for suspending in the roof of the greenhouse, or against an otherwise bare wall.

Dendrobium williamsoni produces several new growths in a season, and from a modestly sized plant can be quickly grown into a fine specimen, which will bloom freely from the previous year's pseudo bulbs.

As with all *Dendrobiums*, they enjoy considerably light conditions combined with a high humidity which is difficult to achieve indoors, and for these reasons they are not always successful as house plants. While good growth can be obtained, they become reluctant to flower.

Dendrobium infundibulum

This is another cool growing *Dendrobium* which was introduced from India in 1862. It is an erect growing plant, and belongs to a group of evergreen species which are distinguished by their black haired stems. Although not a very variable species, it has a variety which shows differences in the shape of the lip, this is *D. infundibulum* var. *jamesianum*. At one time it was considered to be a separate species, along with another variety, *formosum*.

Dendrobium infundibulum is an easy plant to grow provided it be given plenty of water combined with light, moist conditions during the summer, growing months. In its natural state it may become deciduous during the dry season, although under cultivation it remains an evegreen, nevertheless requiring a completely dry rest in the winter. The flowers appear from the topmost parts of the previous years pseudo bulbs, usually two to three from a node. These are large and showy and very long lasting. The papery white flowers are enhanced by the deep yellow stain in the throat of the lip.

Species from this group will not breed with those from the *nobile* type. Their hybridisation is therefore restricted and of little importance. The species in this group are the most beautiful and interesting plants which are cultivated for their own sake.

There are also a number of other white flowered *Dendrobiums* closely related to this species which can be found as far away as the Philippines, although none of these are quite as easy to cultivate in Britain as *D. infundibulum*. Recent conservation laws forbidding the exportation of wild orchids from India will make this and other beautiful orchids rare in cultivation unless they can be raised easily from seed. This would no doubt mean an increase in the cost of producing the plants which would become comparable with the hybrids.

Dendrobium wardianum

This is another very beautiful *Dendrobium* related to *D. nobile*. It first appeared from Assam in 1856, and later a longer stemmed variety, which we know today, came from Burma in 1875. This later introduction confirmed the name of *Dendrobium wardianum*. Previously the plant was considered to be a variety of another *Dendrobium, D. falconeri*. It became immensely popular, and was imported in its thousands.

The culture of *Dendrobium wardianum* is as for *D. nobile*, although it is completely deciduous in cultivation. It blooms early in the year from the previous season's bulb and commences its new growth about the same time. It can be grown in a pot, when the long cane-like bulbs will require the support of a bamboo cane. Or, as an alternative and attractive method of cultivation it can be hung from a basket or wooden raft when the plant can assume its natural downward habit. A number of very early hybrids were made from this species which are hardly seen today. The species is still possible to obtain from the wild, although it will surely become increasingly rare in the future, when the only specimens will be from nursery raised seedlings. Owing to its great beauty it is unlikely that it will disappear altogether from our collections, but will undoubedtly become more expensive as much more time will be required to raise seedlings.

As with *D. nobile, Dendrobium wardianum* also has an albino form. This variety is *D. wardianum* var. *album*, it is totally white and very beautiful.

D. wardianum and a number of related species produce very soft foliage which is particularly susceptible to attacks by red spider mite, more so during the late summer when the pest is most active. As a prevention the plant should be treated regularly with a systemic insecticide.

Dendrobium amethystoglossum

This charming and dainty species comes from the Philippine islands. It produces a multitude of flowers which hang on clustered stems from the older canes.

It was introduced into Britain in 1872 when it appeared in an importation of *D. taurinum*, another species of the same group. The plant was therefore rare in cultivation for many years until it was located in the wild. Today, it is in plentiful supply, and can be grown in the intermediate to hot section of the greenhouse. Most important is that it receives high light, requiring a minimum of shade during the summer months. The plant is an evergreen and retains the majority of its foliage through the winter while at rest.

Dendrobium amethystoglossum does not lend itself to hybridising and no recorded hybrids have been produced from it.

While the plant is typical of the genus in appearance and its cultural requirements are standard for the type, its individual blooms and flowering habit are distinct from the previously illustrated species. While each bloom is small and trumpet shaped, in the massed spikes they are extremely attractive, and many spikes are easily produced throughout the extended flowering season. The stout, upright growing bulbs are best suited to pot culture, where they need only the occasional tie to be kept in place. This suits them better than being grown in baskets, as preferred by many other *Dendrobiums* which have pendent habits.

Dendrobium superbum

This is a truly splendid species from the Philippines from where it was originally imported in 1840. It likes to be grown in hot, humid conditions during the growing season, with a minimum temperature of 65 °F (20 °C). this temperature should rise considerably during the daytime, while the winter temperatures will be slighlty lower. It is a deciduous species, and should be given a completely dry rest when the foliage has been discarded during the autumn. The flowers appear the entire length of the bulb during the following spring, about the same time as the new growth commences. The richly coloured flowers smell strongly of rhubarb.

Dendrobium superbum produces considerably long pseudo bulbs, which can be supported if pot grown, but becomes more attractive when grown in a pendent position from a piece of bark or wooden raft or basket.

A handful of primary hybrids were produced from *Dendrobium superbum* although these were not continued along pacific breeding lines. Now these early hybrids have all passed into obscurity while the species remains a well favoured plant among the hot house orchids.

Dendrobium superbum has an albino variety, *D. superbum* var. *album*, which produces all white blooms. It is considerably rare and beautiful.

This is one of the many fine, closely related *Dendrobiums* which inhabit the Far East and can be found hanging from the trees with their long, slender bulbs no thicker than a pencil, up to 4 feet (1½ metres) long. While resting in their deciduous state they may remain quite unnoticed until they burst into flower filling the surrounding jungle with their heavy perfume.

Dendrobium spectabile

Among the large and varied genus of *Dendrobium*, the species *D. spectabile* can be considered as one of the most curious plants in cultivation. It comes from New Guinea, the home of many extraordinary orchids which have evolved in this remote part of the world.

The plant has a close relative in *D. macrophyllum*, which produces smaller, yellow coloured flowers. This species was introduced from Java in 1846, but is not now in general cultivation. We can assume that *D. spectabile* was introduced at some later date. Both these species have always been extremely rare, and today nursery raised plants of *D. spectabile* are sometimes available. A few sporadic hybrids have been raised from these species, such as *D.* Woodlawn raised in 1950 using *D. spectabile* and *D. atroviolaceum*, the latter being another extraordinary species from the same group which also comes from New Guinea. The flowers of *D. atroviolaceum* will last in perfection for no less than six months!

Dendrobium spectabile is a jungle plant, and enjoys the hot humid conditions consistent with the elevation of the jungles. It is an evergreen which is slow growing and should not be allowed to become completely dry for long periods. It should be kept only partially dry during its resting period, which can be considerably prolonged. It is not unusual for it to remain in a dormant state for a year, or longer, during which time it may flower. Great care should be taken during these extended resting periods with the watering, which should only be given if the plant show signs of undue shrivelling.

Maxillaria grandiflora

The *Maxillarias* are a very large and varied genus of epiphytic orchids coming from tropical America. The majority of these are from Brazil. Many of the species are in general cultivation today, although hybrids are very few and far between. Their flowers resemble those of the *Lycastes* to whom they are closely related.

Maxillaria grandiflora, as the name suggests, is one of the larger and more spectacular members of the genus. The plants can become considerably robust, with tall, broad leaves growing from rather squat pseudo bulbs. The plant flowers freely during the spring months, each flower spike carrying a single, long lasting bloom. Often the plant will bloom two or three times during its extended flowering season, producing several flowers at each blooming.

This species is a native of Ecuador and Peru, introduced about 1850. It grows at high altitudes, and therefore succeeds extremely well in the cool greenhouse. During the winter months it will have a partially dry rest and should be watered only occasionally. When the flower spikes appear, these emerge from the base at right angles to the plant when care should be taken to avoid getting them wet.

Angraecum philippinense

This is an extremely small and graceful species which comes from the Philippine islands and has not been in cultivation for many years. The plant is included among the genus *Angraecum*, although it is correctly *Amesiella philippinense*, this genus having been created especially for this one plant.

Among the *Angraecums* it is not, understandably, typical. Its small compact habit and neat growth make it quite unique. The plants remain small, seldom carrying more than three leaves at one time. It blooms freely during the winter months, producing a short spike of one or two flowers.

The species is best suited to culture in the hot section of the greenhouse where it requires similar conditions to the *Phalaenopsis*, or a well heated indoor growing case. Being of small stature it must be constantly checked to ensure that it does not become too dry at any time, at the same time avoiding overwatering at all costs.

The plant resembles the *Angraecums* with which it has become confused in the characteristic spur which is an extension of the lip and contains the nectar. This factor combined with the pure white colour would indicate that it is probably pollinated by a specific night flying moth.

It is a species which is not plentiful in cultivation, but is well worth growing as a collectors item where suitable conditions can be found for it, requiring little room on the bench.

It can also be grown successfully in a piece of tree branch as illustrated, where it benefits from the high humidity in the greenhouse, while remaining slightly drier at the roots.

Lycaste aromatica and deppei

The *Lycastes* are a most attractive genus of mainly epiphytic orchids coming from tropical America, where they are to be found growing at high altitudes. They produce large, soft foliage which lasts for one season only and is then discarded by the plant. The flowers are produced freely on a single stem from the base of the leading bulb.

Lycaste aromatica and *L. deppei* are two of the most popular among this genus. *L. aromatica* is beautifully fragrant as the name implies. The two species bloom during the spring and early summer months, about the same time as the new growth appears. The plants enjoy cool house culture, and should be kept fairly well shaded during the summer months. During this time the plants are growing fast, and can be given liquid feed at regular intervals. This should be watered into the pot and not given as a foliar feed. The leaves, being extremely soft and papery will quickly become spotted if allowed to get wet.

As the growing season comes to a close with the completion of the bulbs, the plants will shed their leaves, which will slowly turn yellow prior to dropping off. From this time the plants will require full light to ripen the completed bulbs with no water until the new growth is seen the following spring. This winter treatment is important for successful flowering.

L. aromatica and *deppei* were both imported from Mexico in 1828, being strikingly different in their flowers, they make excellent varieties to be grown together. Their ease of culture and free flowering ability make them good subjects for the beginner.

Lycaste Virgo

There has always been great interest shown in the hybridising of *Lycastes*. The opposite species have figured predominantly, as also the species, *L. virginalis*, one time known as *L. skinnerii*. This is a pink and white variety which produces large flowers. The *Lycastes* will also cross with other members of their sub tribe, the *Anguloas* being the most successful. The resulting genus of this cross becomes *Angulocaste*.

   Lycaste Virgo is a three generation hybrid which incorporates three species. These are *L. deppei*, *L. virginalis*, and a green flowered species, *L. locusta*. L. Virgo shows much of the colouring of *L. deppei* while the other species have considerably improved the shape L. Virgo was registered by Wyld Court Orchids in 1970, it is an excellent modern hybrid which has combined the good qualities and vigour of the three species. The hybrids require the same treatment as the species in this genus.

Lycaste Aquila

This is one further example of a good modern *Lycaste* hybrid. The rich, unusual colouring of the flowers has come from a combination of species which have each contributed to the overall result of the hybrid. The species include the highly variable *L. virginalis, L. macrobulbon*, which is a yellow flowered species similar to *L. aromatica. L. lasioglossa* a fine reddish brown species and the green flowered *L. longipetala.*

From the illustration it can be seen that this hybrid has retained last years foliage throughout the winter resting period. The new growths can be seen below the flowers. For exhibiton purposes, the old foliage if spotted with age is usually removed from the plant which increases the effect of the flowers. It should also be noted that this specimen is still a young plant which is producing six flowers. One outstanding feature of many of these *Lycaste* hybrids is the sheer profusion with which they bloom. It is not unusual for a mature plant to produce twenty flowers from a single leading bulb in one season.

It can be seen that the plant in the illustration has become pot bound, and there is no room for the plant to make any more growth in its present pot. Therefore immediately the flowers have finished it will require repotting into a larger pot. Room should be left for at least two more bulbs of the same size as the present one. If done in the spring, the new growth will have the remainder of its growing season to expand its roots.

Anguloa ruckeri

The *Anguloas* are a small genus of large, stately plants which inhabit the Andes at high altitude. They closely resemble the *Lycastes* in their growth and cultural requirements. They are grown today in limited numbers, mainly due to the difficulty of procuring them from their native habitat. Plants in cultivation are more often than not specimens which have been nursery raised from seed. It is perhaps for this reason that more emphasis is placed upon raising hybrids, particularly the intergeneric hybrids with *Lycastes* to produce new and exciting orchids, rather than the pure species which is less interesting by comparison.

Among the species which are grown, about three stand out as being the most striking. All produce large, tulip shaped flowers with the the petals and sepals not opening fully, but held cupped around the lip, which is loosely hinged enabling it to be rocked back and forth inside the flower. It is this unusual feature of the *Anguloas* which has earned them the name of 'Cradle Orchids'.

A. clowesii is perhaps the best loved of the *Anguloas*, noted for its large, bright lemon yellow flowers which are strongly scented. *A. uniflora* is a smaller, almost all white variety, which is lightly spotted with pink on the inside of the flower. This is also fragrant. The illustration shows the most colourful of the genus, *A. ruckeri*. This fine plant produces large, well cupped flowers which are basically olive green, but this colouring is almost obscured by the heavy dark red spotting of the inside of the highly fragrant flower. Several flowers can be expected from a mature plant, appearing about the same time as the new growth. The illustration shows the new growth already higher than the flowers, indicating that this growth was commenced before the appearance of the buds. *A. ruckeri* was reported from Colombia in 1846.

When these beautiful orchids are crossed with *Lycastes*, the flowers become much wider and can be very large and extremely showy. However, they grow into considerably large plants, and when in full leaf require considerable room in which to grow.

Barkeria spectabilis

The genus of *Barkeria* is very similar to, and often included among the *Epidendrums*. The *Epidendrums* are a huge genus of extremely variable orchids which in turn are related to the *Cattleyas* and other allied orchids. While botanically included in the *Epidendrums, Barkerias* are accepted separately for the registration of hybrids within the group. Hybridising of them has been non existent until recently, when a few experimental novelty crosses have been recorded under the new genus of *Bardendrum* (*Barkeria* and *Epidendrum*). These sparse hybrids, however, are not in general cultivation at the present time.

Barkeria spectabilis has a number of other names by which it has been, and in some cases still is, known. These include, *Epidendrum spectabile, Epidendrum melanocaulon, Epidendrum whartonianum*, as well as *Barkeria lindleyanum* and *Barkeria melanocaulon*. This multitude of names probably arose through the species being extremely variable. It occurs in Mexico, Guatemala, Honduras and Costa Rica, and different geographical forms can be obtained from these countries.

Barkeria spectabilis does best when grown in the intermediate section of the greenhouse. It thrives on humidity and during the growing season produces a number of stout, aerial roots from its base. These roots do not generally enter the compost and can be regularly sprayed whilst active. The plants produce modestly sized canes which bloom on completion early in the summer. It is after flowering that most of the roots are made. Towards the onset of winter the meagre foliage is shed, and the roots cease their activity. From this time on the plant can be rested in full light until the following spring when new growth will commence. The plants are at their best when grown in open slatted baskets of small size, or attached to a small piece of bark. At no time should the plants be overwatered, and their container should always be as small as possible.

Coelogyne cristata

The *Coelogynes* are a splendid genus of epiphytic orchids containing a large number of very variable species which are widely distributed throughout the east. Most of them are cool growing, and many make excellent plants for the beginner. The majority of them are easy plants to cultivate, and bloom freely during the spring and summer months. A number of the more showy species are in cultivation, being at the time of writing easy to procure. *Coelogynes* produce pseudo bulbs which vary greatly in their size and shape, with usually a pair of fairly broad leaves. The flowers mostly appear from the new growth when young.

Normal, cool greenhouse or indoor culture will suit them well, in a position of limited shade. During the summer growing season they can be given sufficient water to keep them evenly moist throughout. Upon completion of the season's bulb, they must be rested for the duration of the winter months. During this time they may be placed in full light and allowed to become completely dry. Watering is only commenced as the new growth appears.

Coelogyne cristata is an old time favourite of orchid growers since it was introduced from northern India in 1837. It was grown extensively for its flowers, which were greatly valued for decoration, and has remained a firm favourite since. It will flower regularly if given a good winter's rest and watered well throughout the summer. It is one of the showiest of the *Coelogynes*, producing its beautiful, crisp white flowers from the base of the previous year's bulb, and not from the new growth.

Coelogyne corymbosa

Among the *Coelogynes* white is the most predominant colour although other colours such as yellow, green and brown are not uncommon. However, even among the white flowered varieties there is a great variation to be found in the size and shape of the flower as well as the delightful markings and colours of the lip.

Coelogyne corymbosa is a delightful plant of modest size which blooms profusely during the spring months, when its charming white flowers will last for several weeks in perfection. These appear on short spikes, often attaining a pendent or arching position. It will easily produce several new growths per season and can quickly be grown into a large specimen plant. Even so, it will not require an excessively large pot, and rarely becomes unmanageable due to its size.

As long as these *Coelogyne* species are obtainable from the wild, they will continue to flourish in cultivation. Many of them do not readily breed and seedlings are often difficult to raise artificially. Hybridising within the genus has been limited, and there are very few hybrids of note in cultivation today. Fortunately, the majority of the species propagate very easily and their stock can be increased within a comparatively short time.

Pleione formosana and formosana var. alba

The *Pleiones* are a genus of terrestrial orchids which enjoy immense popularity in cultivation where the temperature is sufficiently cool for them to grow. They are related to the *Coelogynes* and where at one time included, in that genus.

The species in cultivation are found in India, where they grow high up in the Himalayas, along the snow line, and on the island of Taiwan. They also occure throughout the mainland of China. They are deciduous plants which propagate and grow extremely quickly, and large pans of them can be achieved from a single bulb within a few years.

They differ from other orchids in their cultural requirements and habits, and are extremely easy to grow. The new growths appear in the early spring, when the buds show themselves almost immediately from inside the new growth. The buds develop at a fast rate and the blooms open and last for about a week. After flowering, the new growth continues to develop throughout the summer. They produce a squat, rounded pseudo bulb with a single leaf. As autumn approaches, this leaf is shed and the bulbs remain in a dormant state for the winter. By this time the pevious years bulb has become completely exhausted and shrivelled, and is removed from the plant at repotting time the following spring. It is unusual among orchids for the pseudo bulbs to last for one season only. The repotting should be done annually, before the new roots begin to show, this may be before or after flowering. Being terrestrial they succeed well in a peat based compost to which has been added a slow release fertiliser. After repotting they should be kept evenly moist at the roots, while keeping the foliage dry. Half pots or pans are preferable to deep pots and the bulbs should sit on the surface of the compost and not be buried in it.

Their temperature requirements are very low, and the average orchid greenhouse would be too warm for them. *Pleiones* succeed well in alpine houses which are kept frost free, outdoor cold frames, unheated conservatories, or cool rooms.

The most popular species among the *Pleiones* is *P. formosana* (above), prized for its large flowers and delicate colouring. The albino form of this, *P. formosana* var. *alba* (below) is equally sought after, although this variety is rarer than the type. Some very beautiful hybrids have been produced from the limited species available, and these show increased vigour, as well as deeper colouring.

Encyclia radiata, cochleata, mariae and citrina

The *Encyclias* are an extremely pretty genus of epiphytic orchids which were until recently included in the dominating genus of *Epidendrum*. The *Encyclias* shown here are four examples of the variation to be found among the species of the genus. All are easy plants to grow in a cool greenhouse, or indoors.

Encyclia radiata to the left of the picture carries its flowers on upright spikes with the lip held uppermost. The flowers are beautifully fragrant and long lasting. There are a considerable number of similar, closely related *Encyclias* which produce cream coloured flowers of this design. This species flowers early in the summer and comes from Honduras.

Encyclia cochleata illustrated right, has the distinction of being the first species of the genus (*Epidendrum*) to bloom in Europe. Today, it is an extremely popular species among amateur growers, being an easy plant to grow. It blooms at various times of the year, and on a well established, large plant it becomes perpetually flowering. One mature flowering stem will produce a succession of green and black flowers which will continue to flower for over 12 months. By this time a further bulb will have commenced flowering and the plant is never out of bloom. This species often referred to as the 'cockleshell orchid' comes from Mexico and Guatemala.

Encyclia mariae is a truly delightful species and shown in the centre of the group. It is a plant of small size which carries extremely large flowers by comparison. These are produced in the late sping from the previous season's pseudo bulb. The plant requires a decided rest during the winter, and should be watered sparingly during the summer. It makes an ideal subject for growing on wood, which it seems to prefer to pot culture. It is a native of Mexico.

Encyclia citrina can be seen at the bottom of the group. This plant should always be grown on bark and allowed to grow downwards which is its natural habit. The beautiful, deep yellow flower is produced from the previous season's bulb during the spring months of the year. It has a strong fragrance and will last for up to three weeks. The plant likes to be grown always on the dry side, with a completely dry rest during the winter. It does not make an extensive root system and cannot cope with excessive moisture around its base. It is an extremely cool growing species, and is intolerant of high temperatures. It is at its best when grown in the *Odontoglossum* house in a position of good light. Until recently this species was included among the *Cattleyas*.

Encyclia nemorale and brassavolae

This illustration represents two further *Encyclias* which are quite distinct from the previously mentioned species, and which show the vast differences between species of this genus.

Encyclia nemorale illustrated at the top of the picture is most suitable for the intermediate section of the greenhouse or a fairly warm room where there is an abundance of good light. The plant carries two thick leaves to each bulb and a tall flower spike which is produced in the spring. It is extremely variable and at one time several named varieties were known. The plant should be kept well watered during the summer growing season, and allowed to rest when the season's growth has finished. The plant comes from Mexico and is a noble addition to a mixed collection.

Encyclia brassavolae seen at the bottom of the photograph is a vigorous grower for cool greenhouses. It comes from Guatemala where it is found growing at extremely high altitudes. It requires to be kept evenly moist during the summer months, with a semi dry rest while it is inactive during the winter. Often, however, the plant will remain in growth throughout the year, in which case it is watered slightly less in the winter. Its ease of culture and good looking appearance make it an admirable addition to the indoor collection, where it will benefit from the slightly dryer growing conditions. Too much humidity, particularly during the winter months can cause spotting of the foliage, as can too much direct sunlight.

Hybridising among the *Encyclias* has only been achieved to a limited degree. Because many have recently been removed from the genus *Epidendrum*, resulting hybrids between *Encyclias* and *Cattleyas* are named *Epicattleyas*. While hybrids from *Encyclia citrina* (formerly *Cattleya citrina*) are still listed as *Cattleyas*. The earlier classification of the genus being retained for horticultural purposes to avoid even more confusion.

Masdevallia veitchiana

The *Masdevallias* are a very strange and colourful genus which contain many species peculiar to tropical America. They are related to an even larger genus, the *Pleurothallis*, which contain some of the smallest flowers in the orchid family. The *Masdevallias* were quick to gain favour among the early importers and growers of orchids, who could hardly wait to hybridise them. A rush of hybrids were produced, very few of which are in cultivation today. Among the species, the most startling feature is the extraordinary shape of the flowers. The lip, which in the vast majority of orchids is outstanding in at least one respect, has become insignificant in the *Masdevallias* and diminished along with the two lateral petals. The sepals, on the other hand have become grossly exaggerated in their size and very often adorned with long tails.

This species are epiphytic in habit, and produce neat plants which are devoid of pseudo bulbs. The solitary leaves are produced from a short stem at the base of the plant, from where the flower spike emerges. Usually, although there are exceptions, a single bloom is produced on a slender stem, in some varieties these grow horizontally from the plant.

Masdevallia veitchiana is the most striking species within the genus. The bold, colourful flower is held vertically on an extremely slender stem. On a large plant several stems will be produced at a time. It is a plant which propagates readily and grows freely in the *Odontoglossum* house enjoying the cool, shady conditions. This *Masdevallia* was used more than any other in the genus for hybridising. Many fine hybrids resulted around the turn of the century produced by the pioneers of orchid hybridising, James Veitch & Sons, in England. Sadly, none of these superb orchids remain in cultivation today.

However, there is now a renewed interest in these orchids which suffered neglect for years. New breeders are finding that their pollen is extremely small to handle, making pollination difficult, while the seed produced is very fine and of small quantities.

Masdevallia elephanticeps

This species represents one of the more extraordinary rather than beautiful members of the genus. It originated from Colombia and blooms during the spring and summer months. The flower is large for the genus, although the sepals are joined at their base giving the flower a trumpet shape. The diminutive lip is almost black in colour and hairy. It is loosely hinged, and its position can be moved by the slightest touch. This lip movement is a strange and unusual characteristic among the *Masdevallias*. In one species, *M. muscosa*, the lip is sensitive to the extent that it will snap shut when an insect alights upon it. This is an extremely rare occurence among orchids.

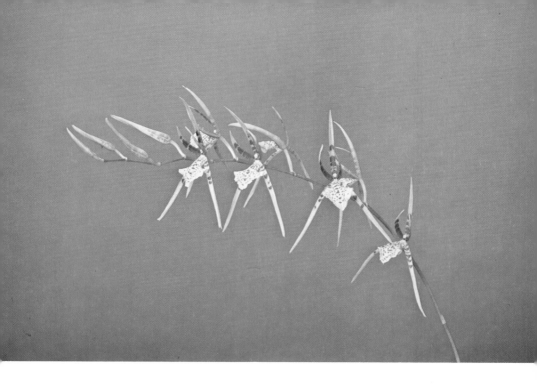

Brassia maculata

The *Brassias* are a genus of epiphytic orchids closely allied to the *Odontoglossums* and other members of the sub tribe *Oncidinae*. They all come from tropical America, and differ from the other genera in the distinctive shape of their flowers. All the varieties have distinctive flowers, with narrow tapering petals and sepals, while the predominant colour is green.

Brassia maculata is among the most popular and showy of the cool growing *Brassia* species. It grows into a handsome plant, and blooms freely during the early summer months. It is fragrant, and will last several weeks in perfection.

The plant should be treated as an *Odontoglossum* but can be kept slightly on the dry side during the winter months when it is not growing. The plant produces an abundance of roots, and grows extremely well in a wooden hanging basket, where its aerial roots can make a most interesting spectacle in the orchid greenhouse. If the plant is being grown indoors, it would do better placed in a pot. The dryer atmosphere of a living room is not conductive to the growth of aerial roots which thrive on humidity.

Oncidium crispum

The large and varied genus of *Oncidiums* which have been described earlier in this book along with the *Odontoglossums* and other allied groups, is full of surprises. Apart from the relatively few *Oncidiums* which have been sought out by the hybridisers to produce the intergeneric hybrids which have become so famous, there are many other *Oncidiums* which are appreciated for their own particular beauty and are therefore grown along with other cool house species for their own appeal.

Oncidium crispum is such a species. At one time an abundant plant it was considered to be a very cheap orchid and was apparently overlooked to a large extent by the hybridisers. Today, it is not very plentiful, and good plants are hard to come by. It was introduced from Brazil in 1830. It is not a very variable species, but has several related species, which are similar to it.

It may be grown in the cool house, although it likes slighlty warmer conditions than the *Odontoglossums*. It should therefore be grown at the warmest end of the cool house, or in the intermediate section where the minimum temperature on the coldest of winter nights does not drop below 55 °F (12 °C). It can be grown in a fairly sunny position and should be kept evenly moist for most of the year.

The plant produces a creeping rhizome between each pseudo bulb which makes it an ideal subject to be grown on a block of wood, such as cork bark or tree fern. When this method of growth is adopted, it will enjoy regular spraying of the whole plant to keep the base continually moist.

Cyrtopodium punctatum

This species belongs to a small genus of South American orchids which are seldom seen in collections, but nevertheless are very striking plants to grow, where sufficient room can be found for them in a hot greenhouse. They produce tall pseudo bulbs which are covered in long leaves throughout the growing season. They become deciduous for the winter months, when a slightly cooler position should be found for them, combined with full light to ripen the bulbs. They can attain a considerable size and the old pseudo bulbs carry thorny spikes where the leaves have been shed, making them extremely spiteful and requiring careful handling.

The flower spike emerges from the new growth when it is quite young and grows rapidly, overtaking the growth and flowering on a tall spike during the spring months. The flowers are brightly coloured and last well in perfection.

Cyrtopodium punctatum can be potted approximately every two years, in a standard compost consisting mainly of bark. The plants have a robust rooting system, and plenty of water can be given during the growing season, together with a regular application of liquid feed, to ensure the vigorous growth of the seasons bulb.

These bulbs can be very large when mature and with their long, spreading leaves the plants require as much room as a large *Cymbidium*, although at the end of the growing season the leaves will all be shed. Therefore the culture of this wonderful plant should not be attempted in a confined space. Being deciduous, the soft leaves have a short lifetime of just a few months. They can quickly become spotted if sprayed with water, and are open to attacks from red spider mite, which will thrive on the soft texture of the leaves.

Grammangis ellisii

This is an unusual species which is quite rare in cultivation. It belongs to an extremely small genus of epiphytic orchids which are related to *Cymbidiums* and *Grammatophyllums*. It was at one time included with this latter genus. The species comes from Madagascar and is the only member of the genus which is occasionally seen.

The plant requires hot house culture with a minimum temperature of 65 °F (20 °C), where it will need plenty of room to grow. It should be watered regularly while it is growing and kept on the dry side during the inactive months. The flower spike is produced from the base of the new growth while it is still young. The unusual shaped blooms last for many weeks in perfection.

No hybrids have been produced from this species, and the plants in cultivation are mostly specimens which have been cultivated for a number of years. The plant is evergreen, with attractive, four sided pseudo bulbs. It has to attain a considerable size before it will flower.

Madagascar is an island unique in its flora and fauna, and its orchids are no exception. Many fine species have evolved there in complete isolation from the rest of the world, making them completly unique. It is absolutely essential that these orchids are not allowed to become extinct through overcollecting of loss of their habitat. With the world-wide interest shown in them, such plants as *Grammangis ellisii* should be safe for the future. The plant illustrated was raised from seed by Marcel Lecoufle, a famous orchid grower who specialises in conservation of Madagascan species in France.

Mormodes unicolor

The *Mormodes* are a most interesting genus of orchids which unfortunately are not greatly favoured among amateur growers. They are epiphytites coming from South and Central America. They are related to another rather strange genus, the *Catasetums*. These two groups are similar in that both produce extraordinary flowers, of unusual structure. When the pollen is disturbed, it springs from the flower with amazing speed. A number of the *Mormodes* carry very colourful flowers, usually heavily spotted. *Mormodes unicolor* is a clear, self coloured yellow and carries a delicious fragrance.

The plant should be grown in the hot greenhouse, with a minimum winter night temperature of 65 °F (20 °C), or if indoors an indoor growing case would suit them best. The new growth commences in the spring which grows speedily, the flower spikes appearing from the base when the growth is about half completed. The plant will often produce two flower spikes in one season. By the autumn the season's pseudo bulb is completed, and the foliage will be discarded. From this time and throughout the winter the plant should be left completely dry in a position of full light, until the next new growth is seen the following spring. While it is growing, *Mormodes unicolor* should receive plenty of water, the plant not being allowed to dry out, with regular applications of liquid feed. The soft foliage should be kept dry. Annual repotting is beneficial, and an open bark compost suits it well.

Very often in the wild these plants are found growing on dead or decaying trees. When the tree eventually falls down the orchid population is doomed. Therefore many *Mormodes* and *Catasetums* have to reach maturity quickly from seed, their lifespan being directly related to their decaying habitat. Obviously, this must be limited to a few years at the most. Hybrids between *Mormodes* and *Catasetums* are easy to make and quickly mature and flower. For this reason they deserve more attention from the breeders of today.

Calanthe vestita

The *Calanthes* are a splendid genus of terrestrial orchids which inhabit a wide area of Asia and can be found from Africa to Australia. A number of the varieties are evergreen types, and these produce the smaller, less interesting flowers which are not frequently found in cultivation. By far the showiest among the species are the deciduous varieties, which produce an abundance of flowers during the winter, when they will last for months in perfection.

Calanthes make handsome plants, producing silvery green pseudo bulbs with a number of large, ribbed leaves, which are broad and very soft.

Before the turn of the century these plants were in great demand for their showy flowers, and were probably grown in greater numbers than any other orchid at that time. The Victorians loved them, and used them for decorating their mansion houses at Christmas time. Also a number of hybrids were produced from the species, a few of which can still be found in cultivation today. The plants grow and propagate extremely quickly, which accounts for the extensive collections that were built up years ago.

They are hot house orchids, which have a fast growing season, during which time they should be given copious supplies of water together with liberal amounts of artificial feed. High temperatures, and a fairly shady position for the summer growing season will suit them well. By the autumn, the leaves will have become old and spotted with age, and will shortly be shed by the plant. From this time on, although the plants will now commence the production of their flower spikes, they should be given no water whatsoever and allowed a complete rest in the hot house where a minimum winter night temperature of 65 °F (20 °C) is maintained. Once the flowers have been removed, the bulbs can be stood on a shelf close to the glass where they will benefit from the full light until their growth commences in the spring. At this time repotting will be necessary, and the bulbs can be potted singly to encourage extra growth. This annual dividing of the bulbs into single ones is contrary to the usual practice of leaving orchid plants in clumps. However, *Calanthe* bulbs are not long lived and become exhausted within two seasons.

Calanthe vestita was introduced in 1848. Several coloured varieties were classified, and many hybrids were raised from it.

Trichoglottis philippinensis var. brachiata

This unusual species represents the little known genus of *Trichoglottis*. These are a group of very interesting orchids which inhabit a large area extending from India to the Philippine islands, with a few species in Indonesia and New Guinea. They are all orchids which require fairly bright conditions in the hot house, where they thrive in the warm, moist atmosphere also enjoyed by the Vandas. Their growth is monopodial, and their leaves are neatly arranged along the upward rhizome. The flowers are short stemmed, and appear singly during the spring and summer months.

Trichoglottis philippinensis is one of the more exciting species, and in the variety *brachiata* the flower is a most unusual vivid colour which is very striking, at the same time being slightly fragrant. The method of growth adopted by this plant makes it an ideal species for novelty potting. Aerial roots are produced throughout its length, as can be seen in the illustration. The most important requirement of this plant is therefore a high humidity. Often, no basal roots are made at all and a pot is merely used to contain the plant, which can look far more attractive and natural on a piece of cork bark or tree fern.